Library of
Davidson College

NEW ENGLAND REVIVALS.

NEW ENGLAND REVIVALS,

AS THEY EXISTED

AT THE CLOSE OF THE EIGHTEENTH,

AND THE

BEGINNING OF THE NINETEENTH CENTURIES.

COMPILED PRINCIPALLY FROM NARRATIVES

First published in the Conn. Evangelical Magazine.

BY BENNET TYLER, D. D.

PRESIDENT AND PROFESSOR OF CHRISTIAN THEOLOGY IN THE
THEOLOGICAL INSTITUTE OF CONNECTICUT.

Prepared for the Massachusetts Sabbath School Society, and
revised by the Committee of Publication.

Richard Owen Roberts, Publishers
Wheaton, Illinois
1980

PUBLISHED IN 1846
BY THE MASSACHUSETTS
SABBATH SCHOOL SOCIETY
OF BOSTON

REPRINTED IN 1980
BY RICHARD OWEN ROBERTS, PUBLISHERS
WHEATON, ILLINOIS 60187

Printed in the United States of America

PREFACE.

The publication of the Connecticut Evangelical Magazine was commenced in the year 1800. It was at a time when God, in a remarkable manner, was pouring out his Spirit on the churches of New England. Within the period of five or six years, commencing with 1797, it has been stated that not less than one hundred and fifty churches in New England, were visited with times of refreshing from the presence of the Lord. Narratives of quite a number of these revivals were published in the early volumes of the above mentioned Magazine. "These narratives," says Dr. Porter, in his "Letters on Revivals," "were written with leisure and deliberation, after the excitement, connected with such scenes of thrilling interest, had subsided. Generally, they were written two or three years, and in a few cases, four years after the revivals respectively were at their height; but rarely within the first year. These papers differ in length, from two or three, to twenty or thirty, close octavo pages; prepared with evident marks of candor and care, with great simplicity, and with a uniformity of statement truly remarkable as to the main characteristics of the work which they record." They were read with great interest and profit at the time of their publication; and they form a chapter in the history of the church, which cannot fail to interest the friends of Zion of the present and future generations. It is obviously important, therefore, that they should be republished, especially, as the works in which they originally appeared, are now but little known, and cannot be easily obtained. This consideration has induced the compiler to give this volume to the public.

The publication of all these narratives entire, would have swelled the volume to a larger size than was judged expedient. Selections have, therefore, been made, and most, if not all of them, have been more or less abridged;—some of them very considerably abridged. In making these abridgments, the compiler has been careful that the sense of the writer should, in no case, be altered or obscured, or the narrative be sensibly interrupted. He has barely omitted such portions as he thought could best be spared, solely for the purpose of diminishing the quantity of matter.

The revivals whose history is given in these narratives, are a specimen of the revivals generally which occurred at the same period, and during the first quarter of the present century. In their origin and progress; in the means used to promote them; in the exercises of the subjects, both previous and subsequent to conversion; and in the permanency of the fruits, there was a striking resemblance. This, so far as it is to be ascribed to any human cause, was doubtless owing to the fact that great harmony of views prevailed among the ministers under whose labors these revivals occurred. They preached the same doctrines, and adopted very much the same measures. It is not surprising, therefore, that the blessing of God on their labors, should produce the same results. True religion, indeed, is the same everywhere, and at all times; and when the same means are used to promote it, we are to expect that its manifestations will be essentially the same.

The revivals of those days were eminently pure, as time has abundantly evinced, and eminently salutary in their influence upon the churches, and upon the community at large. Those who openly espoused the cause of Christ, generally, adorned their profession. There were but few apostacies among them. They were stable, consistent, exemplary Christians. "They continued steadfast in the apostles' doctrine, and in fellowship, and in breaking of bread, and in prayers." These revivals were not temporary excitements, which, like a tornado, sweep through the community, and leave desolation behind them; but they were like showers of rain, which refresh the dry and thirsty earth, and cause it to bring forth "herbs meet for them by whom it is dressed." Their fruits were permanent. By them the churches were not only enlarged, but beautified and strengthened; and a benign influence was exerted upon the community around. Many who were not renewed by Divine grace, were laid under powerful restraints—the tone of morals was elevated—the public conscience was quickened, and a strong conviction was produced in the minds of the great mass of the impenitent, that religion is an all-important reality.

The ministers, whom God employed as instruments in these revivals, were, as a class, excellent men. "Most of them," says Dr. Porter, "I personally knew—many of them were my fathers in the sacred office, whom I regarded then, as I do now, with sincere respect, and veneration. Many of them, were among the most intelligent, and able men of their time." They were generally men of deep and ardent piety, who had " power with God," who loved the souls of men, and who were willing to spend, and be spent in the service of their Divine Master. They were sound in the faith, and shunned not to declare all the counsel of God. They were also men of great practical wisdom. They were not wanting in zeal; but theirs was not a blind, rash zeal which defeats its own object, but a zeal according to knowledge.

They were aware of the fanaticism and delusion which succeeded the "Great Awakening" in the days of Whitefield and Edwards, and of their disastrous influence upon the churches. They were not ignorant of the disorders which prevailed in those days, and the human devices resorted to by misguided zealots which excited the disgust of intelligent, unsanctified men, and strengthened their prejudices against all experimental religion. All these things they carefully avoided. They adopted no measures, suited only to produce excitement; for they believed that all religious excitement is injurious, which is not the result of clear apprehensions of Divine truth.

The means which they employed, were the means enjoined in the Scriptures, such as the plain and earnest preaching of the gospel, and the faithful discharge of all the duties of the pastoral office.

The men of whom we are speaking, dwelt much, in their preaching on the doctrines of grace—such as the entire depravity of man by nature—the necessity of regeneration by the special agency of the Holy Spirit—justification by faith alone—and the sovereignty of God in the dispensation of his grace. They had no fears that the preaching of these doctrines would hinder the progress of a revival. They had the most satisfactory evidence to the contrary. They knew that these truths were suited to quicken and comfort saints, to awaken thoughtless sinners, and especially to guard the awakened against false and delusive hopes. But while they laid before sinners their utterly lost condition, and showed them their entire dependence on the sovereign mercy of God, they at the same time set before them their obligation to obey every Divine command—demolished all their vain excuses, and pressed upon them with great plainness, the duty of immediate repentance. Under such preaching awakened sinners were brought to see their true character and condition. They saw that their hearts were, indeed, enmity against God, and hence it became difficult for them to persuade themselves that they had become Christians till a real change had been wrought in them. And when they became the subjects of renewing grace, they were "born into the truth." They saw from their own experience, the truth of all the great fundamental doctrines of the gospel. Hence they were established in the faith, and not easily carried about by every wind of doctrine.

The narratives contained in this volume may be read with profit by all classes of the community. Professors of religion will find in them much suited to lead to " great searchings of heart." Here are discriminating views of Christian experience. True conversion is here seen to be, not a superficial work—not a mere change of outward conduct—not the formation of a purpose to serve God for the sake of escaping future punishment, and obtaining eternal happiness—but a deep, radical change of all the moral feelings. The converts in these revivals, were not made in that easy way, in which many professed converts in more recent times have been made, without any struggle in their minds, and without feeling any sensible opposition to God and the claims of the gospel ;—but they endured great conflicts. They were convinced of sin. They saw the plague of their own hearts, and knew from their own experience that the carnal mind is enmity against God. And they were brought to love, what they were conscious of having previously hated, and to rejoice in the contemplation of divine objects on account of their intrinsic excellency. Their first religious joys did not arise from the hope that they had escaped from danger; for they found themselves delighting in divine objects, before they had any idea that they were interested in the promises of salvation. These accounts, therefore, are pre-eminently adapted to detect

PREFACE. xi

the false hopes of hypocrites—to convince such as know, in their own experience, of no other religious affections than those which are founded in self-love, that their religion is radically defective.

The real Christian, while he contemplates the scenes of thrilling interest which are here recorded, will be constrained to exclaim, "O that men would praise the Lord for his goodness, and for his wonderful works to the children of men." He will also find himself called upon to pray more fervently, and to labor more diligently for the salvation of his fellow men. He will perceive, that although revivals of religion are the work of God, and strikingly exhibit his sovereignty; he "will yet for this be inquired of by the house of Israel to do it for them." Let all who love Zion unceasingly pray, that pure revivals may increase in number and power, till the whole world shall be converted to Christ.

This volume is particularly commended to the attention, and diligent perusal of the rising generation. The compiler was himself a youth, when these narratives were first published; and when he recollects with what interest he read them, and what impressions they made on his mind, he cannot but indulge the hope, that they will be read with profit by youth of the present and future generations. To all the youthful readers of this book, he would say, you have a personal and infinite interest in the scenes here described. A large proportion of those whose experience is here related were in your period of life. If religion was important for them, it is equally important for you. You too have souls of infinite value. You are, by nature, children of wrath even as others. You too, must be convinced of sin, and be brought out of darkness into marvelous light. Without a great moral change you cannot be saved. A large proportion of those who ever experience this change, experience it in youth. Be entreated then, to attend to the things which belong to your peace while it is an accepted time, and a day of salvation. In these narratives you will see what conviction of sin is; and what change of views and feelings is experienced by those who have passed from death unto life. You will see also, what joy and peace are sometimes experienced, even in this life, by those who are truly converted. O come then, taste and see that the Lord is good. Become the cordial friends and disciples of Christ, and you too, shall know from happy experience, that *wisdom's ways are ways of pleasantness, and that all her paths are peace.*

East Windsor Hill, Nov. 1, 1845.

CONTENTS.

CHAPTER I.

An account of a Revival of Religion in SOMERS, CONN., in the year 1797. By the Rev. CHARLES BACKUS...........................17

CHAPTER II.

An account of a Revival of Religion in CANTON, CONN., in the years 1798 and 1799. By the Rev. JEREMIAH HALLOCK.............23

CHAPTER III.

An account of a Revival of Religion in TORRINGFORD, CONN., in the year 1798. By the Rev. SAMUEL J. MILLS.....................55

CHAPTER IV.

An account of a Revival of Religion in NEW HARTFORD, CONN., in the years 1798 and 1799. By the Rev. EDWARD D. GRIFFIN....63

CHAPTER V.

An account of a Revival of Religion in TORRINGTON, CONN, in the years 1798 and 1799. By the Rev. ALEXANDER GILLET........83

CHAPTER VI.

An account of a Revival of Religion in PLYMOUTH, CONN., in the year 1799. By the Rev. SIMON WATERMAN..................92

CHAPTER VII.

An account of a Revival of Religion in GRANVILLE, MASS., in the years 1798 and 1799. By the Rev. TIMOTHY M. COOLEY......112

CHAPTER VIII.

An account of a Revival of Religion in HARWINTON, CONN., in the year 1799. By the Rev. JOSHUA WILLIAMS..................121

CHAPTER IX.

An account of a Revival of Religion in GOSHEN, CONN., in the year 1799. By the Rev. ASAHEL HOOKER.........................142

CHAPTER X.

An account of a Revival of Religion in LENOX, MASS., in the year 1799. By the Rev. SAMUEL SHEPARD.......................149

CHAPTER XI.

An account of a Revival of Religion in FARMINGTON, CONN., in the year 1799. By the Rev. JOSEPH WASHBURN.................160

CHAPTER XII.

An account of a Revival of Religion in NORFOLK, CONN., in the year 1799. By the Rev. AMMI R. ROBBINS......................179

CHAPTER XIII.

An account of a Revival of Religion in BRISTOL, CONN., in the year 1799. By the Rev. GILES H. COWLES.......................192

CHAPTER XIV.

An account of a Revival of Religion in BURLINGTON, CONN., in the year 1799. By the Rev. JONATHAN MILLER..................211

CHAPTER XV.

An account of a Revival of Religion in AVON, CONN., in the year 1799. By the Rev. RUFUS HAWLEY.......................220

CHAPTER XVI.

An account of a Revival of Religion in BLOOMFIELD, CONN., in the year 1799. By the Rev. WILLIAM F. MILLER..................227

CHAPTER XVII.

An account of a Revival of Religion in MIDDLEBURY, CONN., in the years 1799 and 1800. By the Rev. IRA HART................243

CHAPTER XVIII.

An account of a Revival of Religion in BROOKFIELD, VT., in the year 1801. By the Rev. ELIJAH LYMAN.........................268

CHAPTER XIX.

An account of a Revival of Religion in KILLINGWORTH, CONN., in the years 1801, 1802 and 1803. By the Rev. JOSIAH B. ANDREWS..282

CHAPTER XX.

An account of a Revival of Religion in DURHAM, CONN., in the year 1803. By the Rev. DAVID SMITH...........................300

CHAPTER XXI.

An account of a Revival of Religion in WASHINGTON, CONN., in the years 1803 and 1804. By the Rev. EBENEZER PORTER........308

CHAPTER XXII.

An account of a Revival of Religion in CANTON, CONN., in the years 1805 and 1806. By the Rev. JEREMIAH HALLOCK............321

CHAPTER XXIII.

An account of a Revival of Religion in HARWINTON, CONN., in the years 1805 and 1806. By the Rev. JOSHUA WILLIAMS........335

CHAPTER XXIV.

An account of a Revival of Religion in SOUTH BRITAIN, CONN., in the year 1812. By the Rev. BENNET TYLER..................350

CHAPTER XXV.

An account of a Revival of Religion in BRIDPORT, VT., in the years 1813 and 1814. By the Rev. INCREASE GRAVES..............362

NEW ENGLAND REVIVALS.

CHAPTER I.

An account of a Revival of Religion in SOMERS, CONN., in the year 1797. By the REV. CHARLES BACKUS.

In the latter part of February, 1797, a serious attention to religion began in this town, in the congregation under my ministry. It followed a season of awful security; and was not immediately preceded by any unusual dispensation of Providence, either in the town or neighborhood. There was not at that time, any uncommon serious thoughtfulness within fifty miles of us.

The revival was not rapid in its progress; and never became general in the town. Here and there one in different parts of the place, were seriously impressed, within two or three months from the beginning of the work. It continued to increase for almost a year. It then began to decline. A few new cases of serious thoughtfulness have occurred, at short intervals, until the present time.

The awakening began with the youth, and afterwards extended to the middle aged, and to a few that had passed the meridian of life. The greater part of the subjects of this work, were heads of families. More than half of the whole were under thirty-five years of age. Fifty-two persons united themselves with the church within two years from the beginning of this religious appearance; the most of whom professed to have experienced a saving change in the course of this revival.

This awakening was not in a single instance attended with outcry or noise. The subjects of it appeared very solemn while attending public worship, and conferences. In conversation, they complained of their ignorance and stupidity—they wondered that they had not before seen themselves on the brink of everlasting ruin; and expressed a strong desire to be instructed in the doctrines of the gospel, and to be dealt with in the plainest manner. In some, the alarm was but momentary—they soon returned to their former state of carnal peace. In those who appeared to become the subjects of saving grace, their first alarm was followed by a more full discovery of their moral pollution. They confessed that they felt themselves to be enemies to God, and wholly opposed to the plan of salvation revealed in the gospel. They were distressed because they had no proper conviction of their sins, and observed, that while their consciences told them that they should receive no wrong if they were sent to hell, their hearts rose against the justice and sovereignty of God.

The hopeful converts, in general, observed that when divine truth first appeared in a new and pleasing light, they scarcely thought of their personal safety; or whether they were, or were not converted. They discovered a relish for the doctrines of the Bible; and declared that the truths with which they had been contending, were the objects of their present enjoyment. They were abundant in acknowledging, that if gospel grace were not free and sovereign, there could be no hope for such great sinners as they were. They confessed that they had not made any advances, of themselves, towards submission to the will of God; and that if they were his children, he had in sovereign mercy subdued their hearts by his Spirit. None manifested high confidence of their conversion. They felt themselves bound to confess Christ before men; but were afraid lest they should be deluded by a false hope, and should not live agreeably to covenant bonds. It was common for them to say, when conversing about joining the church, "We know not how to refrain from publicly appearing on the Lord's side; but we tremble at the thought of reflecting dishonor on his name, in the eyes of a scoffing world. Yet unworthy as we are, we desire to give up ourselves to God, and to attend on all the ordinances of his appointment. We know that he can enable us to live to his glory, and we pray that we may always feel our dependence on his grace."

It was animating to meet at the Lord's table in this season of refreshing. Old Christians were enlightened from the beginning of this work. It rejoiced their hearts to behold souls flocking unto Christ, and coming to his table. The old and the young appeared to feel the worth, and to taste the sweetness of the Saviour's dying love. The spectators were more numerous than they had ever been; and not a few of them were in tears. In several instances, persons had their doubts removed, and were emboldened to join the church, by what they saw and heard at the administration of the Lord's supper.

The heads of families who were subjects of this work, expressed astonishment that they had lived so long without any just sense of the duty which they owed to their offspring. They resolved by divine assistance, to train up their children in the nurture and admonition of the Lord. When they dedicated themselves and their households to God, "in the assembly of the saints," there were visible tokens of his gracious presence. They carried religion into their houses, and called upon God's name morning and evening, in a social manner.

The hopeful converts were reformed in their lives, and appeared desirous to know and to practice all the duties both of the first and second table of the law. Amidst the declensions which have taken place, there is reason to hope, that a number will to eternity look back with joy on the late happy season, as the day in which they were espoused to Christ.

It is to be expected in the most promising religious appearances, that there will be tares with the wheat. False brethren have mingled with the true, ever since there was a church on the earth. If any professing Christians rest in past attainments, and become habitually indifferent to holy diligence and watchfulness, they make it manifest that their hope is the hope of the hypocrite. It ought not to surprise us, if we see persons of this description become more loose in their lives than ever before. Persons may hear the Word and receive it with joy, from a belief that they are saved from the wrath to come without any relish for the holy beauty of divine truth. These "have no root in themselves," and hence "endure but for a time." They have nothing to secure them against stumbling at the doctrines of the cross, and shrinking from the trials of the Christian life. They are prepared to fall away; and to imbibe some damnable heresy, or to indulge their vicious propensities without restraint, when assaulted by temptations. "Let him that thinketh he standeth, take heed lest he fall." Christ's sheep will hear his voice, and follow him. They will increase in the knowledge of God, and in the knowledge of the wickedness of their hearts. They will watch and pray, and according to their abilities, will labor to promote the interest of pure and undefiled religion. True Christians do not think highly of their attainments. "Forgetting those things which are behind, and reaching forth unto those things which are before, they press toward the mark, for the prize of the high calling of God in Christ Jesus." They are attentive to duty; and in this way give diligence to make their calling and election sure. The first warmth of young converts is but of short continuance. It is soon exchanged for the conflicts of the Christian warfare. The followers of Christ are conducted towards heaven, in a way which teaches them their perfect dependence on the riches of divine grace. In every step of their journey, they are made to feel that believers are *kept by the power of God, through faith unto salvation.*

CHAPTER II.

An account of a Revival of Religion in CANTON, CONN., in the years 1798 and 1799. By the Rev. JEREMIAH HALLOCK.

THROUGH the course of twelve tedious years, before this memorable period, the religion of Jesus gradually declined among us. The doctrines of Christ grew more and more unpopular; family prayer, and all the duties of the gospel were less regarded; ungodliness prevailed, and particularly, modern infidelity had made, and was making alarming progress among us. Indeed it seemed to an eye of sense, that the Sabbath would be lost, and every appearance of religion vanish—yea, that our Zion must die, without an helper, and that infidels would laugh at her dying groans. But the God of Zion, who can do every thing, was pleased to appear, and lift up the standard of the Omnipotent Spirit against the enemy; and to Him be all the glory.

The first appearance of the work was sudden and unexpected, some particulars of which are as follows. The second Sabbath in October, I exchanged with a brother in the ministry. On my return the next evening, I found a young person under deep religious impressions. She told me she was a poor sinner going down to hell; and that her impressions began on the Sabbath in the forenoon, but increased in the afternoon. And in the evening her concern was such that she could no longer keep it secret, though it had been her intention that no one should know it. The next evening, at a conference, there was an unusual solemnity, and many were in tears. The morning following, I found two other youth, with the one first awakened, whose minds were likewise impressed. On the evening of this day, a sermon was preached by a neighboring minister. The meeting was uncommonly full, and the arrows of conviction reached some hearts.

A young man told me he had, the day before,

drawn a number of books, at the library meeting, on profane history, and was determined to spend the following winter in reading them and the like books; but hearing of this meeting, he came thoughtlessly to it, and soon found he had a greater work to do than to read profane histories. He saw he was an undone sinner, and must become reconciled to God, or perish. His distress arose to that degree, that he seemed almost in despair; but was at length brought into God's marvelous light.

After this meeting, about fourteen children and youth were found, whose minds appeared to be impressed. One of them said, "I have been over a precipice all my days, and never saw it until now." The next day, it was affecting to see, by the rising of the sun, awakened youth coming to my house to know what they should do to be saved. In the after part of the day, I visited a number of females in another neighborhood, where these things had been hardly known, and found a remarkable attention. The tear often flowed on the first mentioning of eternal things. In the evening there were found in the neighborhood where the work first began, at a house where a meeting had been appointed, about thirty children and youth, who appeared serious, and some under deep concern. It was indeed an affecting scene, and one particular fact will not soon be forgotten.

A young woman deeply impressed, said to another in the same situation, "Do not weep so, what good can it do? God does not regard such selfish tears as you and I shed." Upon this, the one spoken to took the other by the hand and said, "O, you are trying to quiet me, but you tremble yourself;" which was truly the case.

On the ensuing Sabbath, the work was visible in the house of God; and the conference in the evening was full and very serious. But one week before, matters never appeared darker; but now the marvelous goings of the victorious Lamb were seen and felt. Oh how little we know what is in the secret counsels of Immanuel! The following Monday, when a sermon was preached by a neighboring minister, almost the whole parish came to meeting, and the work appeared to be going on. And it was a day of trembling, even among professors as well as others. It often brought these words to mind, "But who may abide the day of His coming?"

Being asked one evening to visit a neighbor in distress of mind, I received from her the following information. "I was sober and thoughtful when a child, used to attend secret prayer, thought I loved good people, and finally concluded that I was a Christian. But hearing that the work of God had begun among us, I thought it became me to examine on what foundation I stood; when I found I was building on the sand. On Monday night my hope perished." I do not know that I ever saw any one in bodily distress manifest greater anguish. But before morning she found relief, by having (as she hoped) her will bowed and swallowed up in the will of God. She told me the next morning, "I think I can now take care of my family, and do all for the glory of God."

Before the week was out, another came in anguish of spirit, who also had been resting on a hope of his good estate; but now saw himself to be in the gall of bitterness. He expressed himself after this sort—"I see my heart so opposed to God, that I could not be happy were I admitted to heaven; and I should choose rather to be in hell than to dwell with God." Indeed, this was an hour when all seemed to be shaken. But while some found no rest, short of entirely new hopes, others were confirmed.

The next week, on Wednesday, November 1, another sermon was preached by a neighboring brother, when there was but about half as many present as the week before. And we were greatly afraid that all was about to decline and die. This was indeed a trying hour. No fond parent ever watched the fever of his child at the hour of its crisis, when the period of life or death had arrived, with more anxious, interested feelings, than numbers of God's praying friends watched the work of the Spirit at this critical moment. Every symptom of its being fixed and increasing, was as life from the dead; but the thoughts of its going off were more dreadful than the grave. It was not long, however, before it appeared that God had in very deed come to carry on his work among us. And the hearts of Zion's friends were elated with fresh hopes. Those whose minds were arrested, were, for the most part, increasingly impressed; there were also instances of new awakenings. The solemnity of this season cannot be communicated. It is known only by experience.

A brother in the ministry, among whose people the same work had begun, told me that he had seen twenty in a room, the most of them mortally sick, and at the point of death; but that the scene was not so impressive, as to see a house filled with souls in distress, sensible of impending and eternal wrath, and their feet sinking in that horrible pit, from whence there is no redemption. Nature does not afford an adequate comparison to set forth these scenes. They exceed the things of time, as the soul exceeds the body, or eternity exceeds time. "A wounded spirit, who can bear?" The appearance was more like an execution day. An awful silence reigned, unless when it was broken by the cry, "What shall I do to be saved?" But it was not long, before (as we hope) one and another were brought to repentance and faith, and into the enjoyment of the pardon and comfort of the gospel. And to behold poor sinners who were but yesterday on the brink of destruction, and wholly unreconciled to God, now brought to submit to him, and to hear them sing the new song, entirely surpassed all the victories of the most famous kings and generals of our world.

Here I would also mention, that the things which took hold of the mind were plain gospel truths, with which the people had long been acquainted, and had heard with indifference. I heard one say, "I used to think I believed there was a God, but I find I never did till of late." The work was by no means noisy, but rational, deep and still. The rational faculties of the soul were touched, and poor sinners began to see that every thing in the Bible was true; that God was in earnest in his precepts, and

3*

threatenings ; that they were wholly sinful, and in the hand of a sovereign God. In these things, they seemed to themselves and others like those awaked out of sleep. The heart would oppose, but reason and conscience were convicted, and the mouth was shut. The first that you would know of persons under awakenings was, that they would be at all the religious meetings, and manifest a silent and eager attention. What are called the hard sayings, such as the doctrines of total depravity, of the decrees, election, and the like, were popular. Those who were once angry whenever these things were preached, would cease to object when thoroughly convicted, and rather smite on their breasts.

There was a certain man in the place, fifty years of age, who had neglected public worship, and had always been opposed to the things of the gospel, and who for some time was at all the meetings. On a certain evening, the first part of January, I made him a visit with a view to converse with him on the state of his mind ; when he gave me, for substance, the following account. "My mind began to be impressed as far back as September ; but I kept it to myself. Several things seemed to conspire to increase my attention. Sometime in the fall, I thought in my sleep that my daughter, who is dead, came into the room. I knew that she was dead, and said to her, what have you come for? She replied, 'father, I am come to tell you not to be damned.' Though this was but a dream, it tended to increase my concern. A little after this, these particular words, 'Prepare to meet thy God, O Israel,' sounded daily in my ears. But last night my mind was so impressed that I could not sleep. I arose about midnight, and called up my family. We prayed. After which I returned to my bed again, but was equally distressed as before. When the day approached, I arose, and taking my garments to put on, it appeared to me that they were God's, and I trembled to think how I had used God's property. All that I turned my eyes on looked like God's things. When I opened the door, and beheld the world and the rising morning, the appearance was the same. And the view of the terrible majesty of that God, whose were the heavens, and the earth, and all things, so overwhelmed my mind, that it took away my bodily strength. I turned about and fell on my knees, for I had not strength to stand. I thought of poor infidels, that though they made light of these things, yet, if the strongest of them were to see the dreadful majesty of God, which was now discovered to my mind, they would not be able to stand. After I returned into the house, I directly had a view of the preciousness of Jesus. And I could pour out my soul for Christ's dear ministers. Then my mind turned on the cause of Zion. I longed to have it built up, and the present work go on. I thought of the poor heathen, and said, O that the angel with the everlasting gospel might fly through the earth! I could love my enemies, and pray for their conversion; and confess to every one whom I had injured."

This is for substance what he told me at my entering the house, without being asked a question. After a short pause, he added, "I wish you would pray for me that I may be converted, if God can convert me, consistently with his pleasure and glory. If not, I do not desire it. I wish also you would pray for my poor children, that God would convert them; not that they are any better, or their souls worth any more than my neighbors'." The daylight was now gone, and we went to a meeting. The 102d Psalm was sung—"Let Zion and her sons rejoice," &c. After singing, he expressed himself nearly in these words—"O what sweet singing! I never heard such singing before! This is the first happy meeting I ever saw. I never knew what love was before. I used to think I had love, but I find I never had." This was Friday evening. The following Sabbath, the Lord's Supper was administered. He tarried as a spectator, and appeared to be filled with comfort and joy. In the intermission he observed, "This is the first sermon I ever heard." And he remarked, how gloriously it looked to see Zion sitting at the table of Jesus, and praying unto, and praising her King. As he spake much of his precious Jesus, I inquired, "Why do you thus admire him?" He answered, "Because he loved his Father's law." The question was then put, "Do you think that Jesus is a friend to the divine law and government?" His answer was, "Yes, I believe that Jesus has that regard for the law, that rather than see it made void, he would send ten worlds to hell." The question then was, "Do you love him for this?" He replied, "I do." But all this while, he did not speak of himself as though he thought he was converted.

The work was now evidently on the increase. We had lectures every week, mostly preached by neighboring ministers. And here I would mention, that the awakenings in other places, the proclamation from the General Assembly respecting the Sabbath, and the regulations in schools, all seemed to be attended with good effects. Conferences were set up in every part of the parish. All religious meetings became full and solemn—and every week, and sometimes every day would bring the animating news of some one hopefully converted. Indeed, it seemed as if it would be impossible for any thing to stand before the power of God, and that every one must bow. However, dreadful experience proves, that natural men are, indeed, morally dead. They are harder than rocks, deafer than adders, and more stubborn than the sturdiest oaks. That which will break down the rocks, and tear up the obstinate oaks, will have no effect on the carnal mind. As men did not begin this work of themselves, so neither did they support, or carry it on. But as this was the work of the Omnipotent Spirit, so the effects produced proclaimed its sovereign, divine Author. One was taken here, and another there; and often those whom we should the least expect. I have seen some at this time under the most awakening judgments, as thoughtless as ever; and others in full health and prosperity, pricked in the heart.

A certain neighbor, in the course of the winter, had a dangerous epidemical disease, (which was now very mortal among us) come suddenly into his family in a threatening manner. Yet neither this terrible sickness, nor the awakenings of others, could arouse his attention. But after the family were all recovered, this neighbor (as he told me) on a certain morning arose as secure as ever; but on going to his barn as usual, the thought struck his mind that he could not do the least thing without God. He had lived a careless, vain life, and made light of the awakening. He told me he thought it was too silly a thing for rational creatures to attend to. He used to say, if a man labored hard, he ought to live well. Hence he felt no obligation, nor saw any cause even for asking a blessing, or returning thanks. But now when the thought struck his mind that he had no independent power to do the least thing without God, it pricked him to the heart. This infinite God appeared the great, and first cause of every thing, and all centered in Him. He was at first determined to suppress and conceal his convictions, but soon found it impossible. And after about two weeks, he was hopefully brought savingly to submit to God.

Another person told me thus. "I was returning, on such an evening, from a conference, where I had seen numbers under concern, and heard others speak of the love of God, and of their hope in Christ. But nothing took hold of my mind, until as I was on my way home, these words sounded in my ears—'Is it nothing to you, all ye that pass by?' These words were fixed in his mind, and he applied them thus—'Is it nothing to me that my neighbors, and those of my age, are troubled about their sins, and some hopefully converted to God? Have I not sins to be troubled about as well as they? And do not I also need conversion?'" I saw this person about a fortnight after his mind was thus taken hold of, and his convictions were much increased; when he observed thus—"I find that all I do is selfish. If I pray or read, it is all selfish. And I feel myself like one hung upon tenter hooks. His situation is very distressing, but the more he struggles, the deeper the painful hooks penetrate." This was on Saturday, and it was, indeed, a serious, trying hour. But the next day, this man hopes that he received a new heart from the ascended Saviour. I have heard him say, that a new heart, or deliverance from sin, appeared, he thought, more precious than deliverance from hell.

I have observed that this spiritual shower was sovereign in its operation. There was a certain man, between forty and fifty, living in a remote part of the parish, who was a Gallio as to religion, and entirely absorbed in the things of the world. He had attended no conferences, and was seldom at meetings on the Sabbath. But one evening having gone to bed as thoughtless as ever, he awaked about midnight, when these words came forcibly to his mind—"O that they were wise that they understood this, that they would consider their latter end." Here was the beginning of his conviction, which lasted three or four weeks. I have heard him say, that he found himself naked, a sinner, and without excuse. And before he found Jesus, he was brought to see that God was just, if he sent him to hell.

I said in the beginning of this letter, that before the awakening, modern infidelity had made, and was making, alarming progress among us. Some who had been infidels for years, are among the hopeful converts, and are laboring to build up the faith they once sought to destroy. I heard one of them say, with trembling limbs, "I am the wretch who have murdered Christ—I have talked a great deal against the gospel; but there was always something in my breast which said it was true, even while I was talking against it." This poor man was almost in despair. But after a long series of distress, he found comfort.

From another, who had been opposing the divinity of the Scriptures, I received the following letter :

"Rev. Sir—I frequently hear you mention, from your pulpit, that there are numbers in this place who are opposers to Christianity. Doubtless you allude to me for one. If this be the case, you have good reason to make the allusion ; for I frankly confess (not without some sorrow) I have given great reason for such suspicion. It is nearly ten years since I have entertained doubts respecting the truth of revelation, not without a mixture of necessary belief in it, as the only scheme to bring glory to God, and happiness to man. Could I convince you of my sincerity, I doubt not you would be glad, when I tell you I renounce my doubts ; and therefore I pray God I may never more give the world reason to call me an opposer to religion. I have often come to a partial resolution to make you such a confession of my errors. The first time I seriously engaged with myself to do it, was on hearing you read some letters which you brought from Goshen, and your remarks upon them. I then reflected whether it belonged to me to animadvert on the ways of God's providence, and the authenticity of that which, in itself, looked like truth. But afterwards, doubts, and business, and reluctance to part with my favorite schemes, intervened, or you would have had this letter before this time.

"The cause of my writing this letter now is not the fact that religion is becoming fashionable in this place, or any extraordinary conviction on my mind, more than I have had for some time, at short intervals, betwixt my doubts. Which conviction, I think, is nothing more than that it is my duty to serve God in his appointed ways. I pray God he would guard me against doubts hereafter. I beg you to be assured of my esteem."

Here was the beginning of conviction on this person's mind. It, on the whole, appeared gradually to increase about eight months, until it became powerful, and he saw himself wholly depraved, and in the hands of a sovereign God; when, as he hopes, he was made to partake of the joys of the penitent prodigal. I have said the work was not noisy, but rational; and one end I have in transcribing this letter is to give a specimen of it.

There is another instance among us, of one

who says, he has had no trouble for seven years past, about futurity, concluding that death was the total end of man, as much as of the beasts. At first, he made an open scoff and ridicule of the awakening. But, at length, the arrows of truth reached his conscience. His conviction continued and increased for some weeks, until, as we trust, he became reconciled to God through Christ. He now appears to love the doctrines of the cross. Formerly he had a taste for books, and read much in novels, profane history and the like; but now he calls them trash, and makes the Bible his study, and seems to want words to set forth how much it exceeds all other books.

But to proceed to an instance or two more. I was at a certain conference in which the conversation turned on the doctrines of decrees and election; which sublime doctrines were not attended to now for disputation, but with fear and solemnity. They did not appear to be dry, uninteresting, disputable points, but divine realities, calculated to convict the sinner, and refresh the saint.

At the close of the meeting, a certain man asked a question to this import—"Does a person who is truly seeking after God, feel afraid that any of the decrees of God will cut him off from salvation?" This question was answered in the negative; that the decrees were no more against prayer, than an attention to common matters, and that the only reason why men brought the decrees against prayer, was their having no heart to pray. The person who put the question, answered, "I am satisfied." But knowing him to have long been an opposer of these things, many marveled at his answer.

On the next Sabbath, this man made a public declaration in writing to the congregation, which accounts for his appearing to be satisfied with those very doctrines, which used to give him so much offence. In this public confession, he acknowledges his past infidelity, his opposition to God and his religion, to the work of the Spirit, to the ministers of the gospel, and all who profess to belong to Christ. But that God had showed him his sinful, wretched, helpless state, and given him to hunger for the bread of life, and to believe (as he trusted) in Jesus. The writing which he publicly exhibited is in these words:

"It having pleased the kind Sovereign of the Universe to open my eyes, in some measure, to see the depravity and poison of my own heart— to see my desperate situation while opposed to

God, and to the way of salvation by a kind Saviour—to see my total inability to rectify my own heart, or recover myself from the fatal disease of sin and death—to see, if I am ever relieved from the plague of a proud and vitiated heart, and made to rejoice in the salvation of Christ, it must be wholly owing to the forfeited mercy, and unmerited grace of a compassionate Redeemer. With these things fastened on my mind, and, I hope, as long as I live, I would wish to make some communications to this religious assembly, which, I hope, may be kindly received by them. For several years past, my mind and affections have been much alienated from the new and living way of salvation by Jesus Christ. I have fallen into the most uncomfortable doubts of his divinity—have doubted of the authenticity of His blessed Word—have embraced irreligious and hateful errors—have turned my back on the blessed Redeemer, while his friendly hand has reached out a pardon to me, and urged me to take it, even while his head was filled with the dew, and his locks with the drops of the night. I have run away from the blessed God, while his tender mercies were all around me, and with a sweet voice saying unto me, 'Turn ye, turn ye, why will ye die?' I have lived in dreadful security, and stopped my ears to the most melting invitations of the Saviour of the world. I have spent much time in reading books which were calculated to shake my faith in that holy Word, which, had I sincerely believed it, would have given me great comfort in God, and served in a great measure to smooth the rugged path of life. I have been guilty of many errors in sentiment and practice. I have slighted the blessed religion of Jesus Christ, the ministers of the gospel, and professors of religion. I have spoken lightly of the religious attention in this place, and have neglected to attend religious conferences, which by God's Holy Spirit are undoubtedly instrumental of true conviction. I have been given to many open immoralities, and have not been circumspect in my behavior, to set a good example before those who took knowledge of me. And now in every instance wherein I have offended my heavenly Father, and mankind, I would freely acknowledge my great sin, and numerous transgressions, imploring the forgiveness of that Almighty Being, against whom I have unreasonably, and without the least provocation, so often transgressed, and who only can bestow pardon and eternal life on the chief of sinners. It appears one of the most distinguished mercies, that when people have run into error, and marred themselves by sin, that there is a Being to whom they may apply, with broken hearts, and who will blot out their sin with his own blood, and give them to eat of the bread of life. 'He that covereth his sins shall not prosper, but he that confesseth and forsaketh them shall find mercy.' Certainly there can be no exchange so happy as this, to part with a proud and wicked heart for a humble and sanctified one ; to resign our enmity for love, and selfishness for benevolence, our filthy self-righteousness for the spotless robes of a glorious Mediator, and our love of sin and death, for holiness and eternal life.

"With the foregoing considerations on my mind, I will implore a prayer-hearing God to lend a listening ear to my requests, which I pray God to help me make with sincerity. My first desire is for a rectified heart, to have sin slain, and a principle of true holiness and love to God, implanted in its stead, and a heart of constant repentance and unfeigned sorrow for sin. I pray God to grant me all my life, a deep sense of my own unworthiness and ill desert ; I pray to realize it as long as I live ; to lie in the very dust, at the feet of the great Sovereign of the Universe ; to extol, magnify, and glorify the riches of his moral rectitude, his glorious attributes, his infinite perfections ; to entreat of him for Christ's sake, to give me his blessed Spirit, to lead and guide me into all truth, to make me steadfast in a life of religion, to save me from a life of unbelief, from backsliding, and apostacy, and finally to engage me to resolve, in the strength of the Great Redeemer, to take his yoke on me which is easy, and his burden which is light, and learn of him who is meek and lowly, that I may find rest to my soul.

"I hope that God by his great mercy and rich grace, has given me to hunger for the bread of life, and thirst for living water; that he has given me to see that Christ is the way, the truth and the life ; and that there is salvation in no other way. And now before God, and this solemn assembly, and I hope with a broken and sincere heart, I renounce the heart-tormenting, and heaven-provoking principles of infidelity, so dishonoring to God, and pernicious to mankind. But before I close this writing, I must drop a few hints to those with whom I have associated in infidelity for some years past.

"You will not view me as reflecting on you, for I sincerely pity you. I tremble for the fatal mistake you are making. Is deism a good scheme to embrace in death? Is there comfort in it of a happy immortality? Will it make a dying hour serene and joyful? Can you expect to find a smiling God out of Christ? Can you be satisfied that infidel principles are calculated to humble the proud and rebellious hearts of mankind, and to exalt the Most High? Will you not be persuaded to abandon a scheme which excludes prayer, and shuts out all heavenly contemplation? Can you bring up your dear children and never pray to God for them, nor mention a word concerning religion and the great God, for fear their minds may be prepossessed in favor of a scheme, of which, if they had come to riper years, they would discover the fraud, and disbelieve it for themselves? When your offspring come before you, with wishful countenances, asking for bread, does it never turn in your minds about the bread of life?— that their souls are famishing while their bodies are nourished?

"I will mention but one more consideration, and that a dreadful and awful one. You must meet your beloved children before God's bar, and there answer for your conduct towards them. Should they, in consequence of your total neglect to instruct them in religion, be doomed to a dreadful hell, will they not shriek out these heart-rending words, with horrid emphasis, 'Father, you never told me of this dreadful place; you never told me of a glorious escape, a glorious relief by Jesus Christ; and must I lie in this dismal, burning lake! O, unhappy; that you was ever made the instrument of my existence!' Now, will you come to the Saviour, and bring your whole families with you? There is bread enough in our Father's house. I pray God that he will, in great mercy, be pleased to open your eyes, to discern wondrous things in that law which you have rejected, and to see ineffable beauty in that Saviour whom you have disowned."

The above communication was exhibited Lord's day, April 14, 1799, to a numerous audience. Many of them were much affected, and most of the infidels alluded to were present.

The author of the above communication says, that being at meeting on the Lord's day, a number of months after the revival had begun, on hearing the names of ten persons called, who were propounded to join the church, his mind was struck with the cutting thought that an eternal separation was about to take place between people of the same congregation, neighborhood, and family. And as there was room enough, he could see nothing to hinder him from coming to Christ too, but his own unwillingness. These were about the first of his impressions. In the evening, he thought he would go to the conference; but as he had never been to any of the conferences, and had even spoken against them, he felt many objections. Yet he concluded to go at all events. I have heard him say, the first thing that struck his mind, as he entered the house, was the decorum and order of the meeting. His convictions continued and increased for a number of weeks, until he was brought, as he confesseth, to see his desperate situation, while opposed to God, and the way of salvation by a kind Saviour; and to see that Christ was the way, the truth and the life, and cordially, (as he hopes,) to accept of him.

Thus I have given some account of the work of God among us, and mentioned some particular instances in which the nature of the work appears. As to the extent of it, there were but few in the parish who were not, in a measure, solemn. Almost the whole conversation when people were together, in intermissions on the Sabbath, and on week days, was on religion. Even companies, on training days, were solemn. Balls were suppressed, and religion was the theme at weddings, and at all times. The number hopefully born into the kingdom of God is between sixty and seventy. The number who have made a public profession is fifty-nine, and it is expected that others will come forward, and subscribe with their hands unto the Lord. I would here notice that though many have been taken, to human view, the farthest from the kingdom of God, yet I think that God, in the midst of his sovereign, holy ways, must appear, even in this work, to every attentive soul, to be a prayer-hearing God. In the middle of the place, there was, during all the past days of inattention, a praying conference kept up once a week (extraordinaries excepted) by a few serious people. And it was here in this conference, that the work begun, and here it has been the greatest. Surely he is a God who hears the prayers of the destitute.

I shall close by giving a brief account of one who left the world in the height of the attention among us. She died May 15th, 1799, in the sixteenth year of her age. She was a promising youth, of bright natural abilities, and of a respectable religious family. Her mind began to be impressed, the latter part of the year before she died. As she had been taught the ways of the Lord in the family, from her childhood, she appeared early in the awakening to have a good doctrinal knowledge of the way of salvation. But she complained of a hard heart, and a stubborn will. She was at all meetings and conferences which she could conveniently attend; but found no relief. In the latter part of February, she began to be unwell, and was soon confined. Her disease quickly became very threatening; and within a few months she was given over by her physician. But though her bodily disease was distressing, yet it was in a great measure overbalanced by her spiritual troubles. Her complaint was chiefly of her selfish heart, which she felt to be at enmity with God; and the prospect of going out of the world with arms in her hands against the Most High, was horrible beyond conception. She would often in great anguish cry out, " I must die, and I cannot die so." Such a scene, especially in a day of awakening, was very affecting, and it excited the pity and prayers of many. A number of young people who had been under concern, and had obtained relief, went one evening to see her about a fortnight before she died, and conversed and prayed with her. As they were going away, she begged their prayers. And her request and situation were so affecting to them, that they (as I am told) after leaving her, retired, and spent an hour of the silent midnight in carrying the case of their distressed friend to God. And we have reason to hope that on this very night, she received, from the ascended Saviour, the gift of a new heart. There appeared to be a great alteration in her mind from this time; though she had many doubts and fears until the morning before her death, when every cloud seemed to be dispelled. And I can say, I never saw so much triumph and victory in the arms of death before. She expired not far from twelve on Saturday. Her joys had not the appearance of a vain confidence, but of a real submission to God, in view of his glory in the face of Jesus Christ. She possessed her reason perfectly. There was a holy fear mixed with her joy; and though she said many things while she lay dying, yet it was with as much apparent care, as a considerate witness would speak in a case of life and death.

I shall here mention a few of her dying words, which were written at the time of her death. I heard most of them myself, and wrote as she spake them. Not far from sunrise, she expressed herself thus—"I have lived through a tedious night, and am brought to see the light of a glorious morning." Not long after she expressed herself in these words—" Now I am going to Jesus, to be disposed of just as he pleases. I am not afraid to be dead—I am not afraid to die." The house was soon filled with the neighbors, and her young friends. But though death had evidently seized on her mortal body, immortal glory seemed to bloom in her soul; and she knew and kindly received all who came to see her, and spoke discreetly and suitably to them. She looked on one of her mates and said, "Now you see my heart-strings break." On one's asking her if she might not be deceived, it engaged her serious attention, when she replied, "Why I know Jesus will take me; if he does not, he will do me no injustice." As she drew nigh her exit, she rattled in her throat. Being asked if she wished for drink, her reply was, "No, it is nothing but the pangs of death." On seeing her struggles, one of the spectators said, it is hard to die. She answered, "It is hard, you may depend." She calmly looked on her dying fingers, spoke of her grave and funeral, and bid me in her name to tell her young friends and others at her funeral, to learn to die, and that she bid them farewell. In speaking of these things, she was as rational, calm and deliberate, as a kind parent on going a journey would be in giving directions to his family. About three minutes before she died, with a distinct and audible voice, she called two young people (who then came in) by name, saying, "Fare you well; I have almost got through this troublesome world." She seemed to die with a lustre in her eyes, and a glow in her countenance. It was a wonderful scene of death and triumph. I sat before her, and looking her in the face, my heart naturally cried,

> "Hosanna to the Prince of Life,
> Who clothed himself in clay,
> Entered the iron gates of death,
> And tore the bars away."

I blessed that work which issued in such a victory over the king of terrors, and in such a lively hope of immortality, and could not but bless those converted to Christ, and congratulate them in their happy prospects in death.

These things were confounding even to infidels, and numbers who had thought lightly of the work, were now ready to smite their breasts, and say, truly it is of God. I might enlarge, but the time would fail. I have endeavored to state simple facts according to the best judgment of a fallible creature, with a mixture of joy and fear.

When I find Peter, an apostle, deceived in Simon Magus, and hear him when speaking of the faith of Silvanus, using the cautious language, "A faithful brother, as I suppose," it makes me tremble for fear how we shall hold out. We cannot tell what will be on the morrow, and man is ignorant of the heart. Hence my desire is, that all whom I have alluded to in the above narration, will remember that this is not an hour of boasting, but of putting on the harness, and that it still remains to be proved by their fruits, whether they have true religion or not. On the other hand, there is joy and hope in God, and I desire to be thankful to him, that he hath allowed me to stand and behold his glorious work; though I must confess that I never felt so useless since I entered the ministry. God hath wrought, and to his name be all the glory. And may he strengthen his own work, and more abundantly increase it, until all that is, shall, as it were, be absorbed in greater glory.

CHAPTER III.

An account of a Revival of Religion in TORRINGFORD, CONN., in the year 1798. By the Rev. SAMUEL J. MILLS.

IN the latter end of August, 1798, unusual religious appearances commenced in this place, especially among the young people. They met weekly by themselves. Their number constantly increased, until it was found that a private room would not contain them. They then repaired to the meeting-house, where they prayed, sang, and conversed on religious subjects. An event so extraordinary, excited a spirit of general inquiry throughout the society, and several weeks, and even months passed away, while as yet one was scarcely able to decide whether any very deep or powerful impressions were on their minds, or not, unless in a very few instances.

In the meantime an unusual solemnity appeared on the countenances of the people in general. And those who antecedently to all this, had been much in prayer to God for a day of his divine power, thanked God, and took courage. Of course, conference meetings of a more general nature, were appointed ; and crowds were wont to assemble at such seasons.

Thus things passed on, with but few instances of hopeful conversion until about the middle of the following winter.

While our hopes, and our fears, had thus long been sensibly excited, by turns, as appearances varied, at this memorable period, it pleased the Great Head of the church in a very peculiar manner, to show forth his presence and power in the midst of the people. So extraordinary a season, for weeks, and we may say, for months, we never witnessed. An answer to the inquiry whether the Lord was indeed among us, or not, was attended with no difficulty. The minds of many were greatly agitated, and unusual attention was paid to the means of instruction. In the time of this extraordinary visitation, a goodly number of the people obtained hope of their reconciliation to God.

Having made this general statement, I shall now descend to some particular observations.

1. It is worthy of particular notice, that the work has been carried on with remarkable regularity. Little or nothing has been discovered of wild enthusiasm or disorder. The subjects of the work have been as able, and ready in any stage of it, to describe their distress, as a

patient to tell what part of his body was in pain. This, perhaps, may, in a measure, account for the fact that there has been so little open opposition to the work. Such as wished to censure and reproach it, were confounded. It may be observed,

2. As to the nature of the work, that it has been such, in the course and issue of it, as wonderfully to display divine power and grace, and to bring out to view, the human heart. The subjects of it in the first stages of their concern, have generally been filled with surprise, and astonishment at themselves, and their past lives. And seeing themselves in danger, have formed resolutions, and entered on measures to amend their situation. When led to a more full discovery of their own hearts, and to an increasing conviction of the impossibility of ever obtaining relief, in their own way, they have felt very sensibly disturbed. They have been ready to plead in their own defence, while they dared to do it, that they could do no more than they could—that they never made their own hearts—and that it was out of their power to change them. They have contended also against God, for showing mercy to others, while they were left—and even for giving them existence. But as their convictions increased, they became sen-

sible of the dreadful obstinacy of their own hearts, and found themselves growing worse and worse, till finally all hope disappeared, except what arose from the sovereign grace of God—from the consideration that he could, and that he would have mercy on whom he would have mercy. They found their hearts so much opposed to God, and to his law and to his gospel, as to see that nothing short of divine power could ever subdue them. In the midst of all this, their proud and obstinate spirits would rise against that sovereign grace which secured them from utter despair, and contained their only remaining hope of escaping divine wrath. But no sooner were they led to a discovery of the justice of God in their condemnation—to see and to feel that the law was right, and holy, and hell their proper place, than they found their mouths shut, and their complaints at an end. They have readily acknowledged that God would be glorious in executing sentence against them. Thus have they been brought to resign themselves cheerfully, without any reserve into the hands of God, to be disposed of as may be most for his glory—rejoicing that they were, and might lie in the hands of such a holy, just and wise God, let their future situation be what it might. There have been among them, such expressions as these. "The character of God has appeared inexpressibly beautiful, even in the view of his pronouncing sentence against me. I wish that others might praise God, though I should perish."

It has been no uncommon thing for the subjects of the work, whose chief distress and anxiety antecedently arose from a sense of their being in the hands of God, unexpectedly to find themselves rejoicing in that very consideration—contemplating the glory and happiness of God, as an object of higher consequence, and more precious than their personal salvation; and all this, while as yet, they have had no idea of having experienced any saving change of heart.

They have in various instances apparently rejoiced in God's supremacy, and in being at his disposal, calmly leaving their case to his wise and holy decision, and have conversed in a language to which they never before were accustomed, and have gained the favorable opinion of others, while they have had no such thoughts respecting themselves. Instead of this, jealousies have often been excited in their minds, (on finding themselves so calm and peaceful,) that God had left them—that their concern was over, and they have wished it to return again. And when, at length, reflecting on their views and feelings, or by conversing with others, they have ventured to entertain some feeble hope about themselves, it has been in various instances of short continuance. Within the course of a few days, or perhaps a shorter period, they have had such an overwhelming sense of the extreme sinfulness and corruption of their own hearts, as to be ready to conclude it to be utterly impossible that they should have any grace. This may account for a remark frequently made by themselves, and circulated by others, that they had given up their hope.

In consequence of becoming reconciled to the divine character, law, and sovereignty, to which before they were so much opposed, the character and work of Christ have been wont to appear unspeakably glorious, and beautiful, as magnifying the divine law, and opening a way for the acceptance of sinners in such a manner, as glorifies God, and exalts the grace and work of Christ, and lays them prostrate at his feet.

The great and essential difference between their former and present views and feelings, has very sensibly affected their own minds, as well as the minds of others; especially in those instances in which they had antecedently distinguished themselves, by their opposition to the doctrine of decrees, divine sovereignty, the absolute dependence of the creature on God, and his universal providence, and the duties of unconditional submission, and disinterested affection. To find themselves now attached to those very doctrines and duties, and lamenting their former blindness, has served to excite peculiar admiration and gratitude.

3. It may, perhaps, be proper to notice, that the great Head of the church, has by no means confined himself in the display of his grace to persons of any particular rank or age. Children and young people of both sexes, and heads of families, of different ages, and in one or two instances, such as were far advanced in life, are among the number who hope, that though once they were blind, now they see.

The impressions were such on the minds of the children in different schools, as led them to lay aside their customary diversions, and sometimes to pass their intermissions in prayer, reading, or religious conversation among themselves. Such as were capable, requested it as a privilege, that they might be allowed at school to read in their Bibles. Several of the scholars obtained hope respecting themselves—some under twelve years of age; but the greatest number between twelve and eighteen.

4. The uniformity everywhere observable,

as to the views and exercises of the subjects of the work, is a circumstance particularly to be noticed, both antecedent to their obtaining relief, as well as afterwards. Most generally, let any person become informed in respect to a single instance of the views and feelings of a sinner, under concern, and of his consequent exercises, and different views, and apprehensions, and he would for substance learn what others could say. The same excuses, pleas, cavils, and objections against the doctrines and precepts of the gospel, while under conviction, and the same kind of submission, when brought to a cheerful surrendry of themselves to God which were found in one case, were to be looked for in another. To find persons who never conversed, one with another, communicating the same ideas, has been very striking to many. And it ought to be particularly observed here, that this is not the case merely in neighborhoods or societies, but in distant and different quarters, wherever the work has spread, among those who never saw, or heard of each other. The observations already made respecting the nature of the work in this society, apply with equal truth to other societies, so far as can be known, both far and near. All are made to drink into one spirit, and to speak one language.

CHAPTER IV.

An account of a Revival of Religion in NEW HARTFORD, CONN., in the years 1798 and 1799. By the Rev. EDWARD D. GRIFFIN.

THE work of divine grace among us three years ago, by which nearly fifty persons were hopefully added to the Lord, had not wholly ceased to produce effects on the people generally, when the late scene of mercy and wonder commenced. In the interval, several were, in the judgment of charity, "created anew in Christ Jesus unto good works." It is not known, however, that any thing took place in the summer of 1798, which had immediate connection with the present work, unless it were some trying conflicts in a number of praying minds, which appeared to humble and prepare them for the blessings and duties of the ensuing winter.

Late in October, 1798, the people frequently hearing of the displays of divine grace in West Symsbury, (Canton,) were increasingly impressed with the information. Our conferences soon became more crowded and solemn. Serious people began to break their minds to each other;

and it was discovered, (so far were present impressions from being the effect of mere sympathy,) that there had been for a considerable time in their minds special desires for the revival of religion; while each one, unapprised of his neighbor's feelings, had supposed his exercises peculiar to himself. It was soon agreed to institute a private meeting for the express purpose of praying for the effusions of the Spirit, which was the scene of such wrestlings as are not, it is presumed, commonly experienced. Several circumstances conspired to increase our anxiety. The glorious work had already begun in Torringford, and the cloud appeared to be going all around us. It seemed as though Providence, by avoiding us, designed to bring to remembrance our past abuses of his grace. Besides, having been so recently visited with distinguishing favors, we dared not allow ourselves to expect a repetition of them so soon; and we began to apprehend it was the purpose of Him whom we had lately grieved from among us, that we should, for penalty, stand alone parched up in the sight of surrounding showers. We considered what must be the probable fate of the risen generation, if we were to see no more of "the days that were past" for a number of years, and the apprehension that we might not, caused sensations more easily felt than described.

This was the state of the people, when, on a Sabbath in the month of November, it was the sovereign pleasure of a most merciful God very sensibly to manifest himself in the public assembly. Many abiding impressions were made on minds seemingly the least susceptible, and on several grown old in unbelief. From that memorable day, the flame which had been kindling in secret broke out. By desire of the people religious conferences were set up in different parts of the town, which continued to be attended by deeply affected crowds; and in which the divine presence and power were manifested to a degree which we had never before witnessed. It is not meant that they were marked with outcries, distortions of the body, or any symptoms of intemperate zeal; but only that the power of divine truth made deep impression on the assemblies. You might often see a congregation sit with deep solemnity depicted in their countenances, without observing a tear or sob during the service. This last observation is not made with design to cast odium on such natural expressions of a wounded spirit. But the case was so with us, that most of those who were exercised, were often too deeply impressed to weep. Addresses to the passions, now no longer necessary since the attention was engaged, were avoided, and the aim was to come at the conscience. Little terror was preached, except what is implied in the doctrines of the entire depravity of the carnal heart—its enmity against God—its deceitful doubtings and attempts to avoid the soul-humbling terms of the gospel—the radical defects of the doings of the unregenerate, and the sovereignty of God in the dispensations of his grace. The more clearly these, and other kindred doctrines were displayed and understood, the more were convictions promoted. By convictions, are meant those views and feelings which are caused by uncovered truth, and the influences of the Spirit antecedently to conversion.

The order and progress of these convictions were pretty much as follows. The subjects of them were brought to feel that they were transgressors, yet not totally sinful. As their convictions increased, they were constrained to acknowledge their destitution of love to God; but yet they thought they had no enmity against him. At length, they would come to see that such enmity filled their hearts. This was particularly exemplified in a certain house in which were two persons exercised in mind. One appeared to have a clear sense of this enmity, and wondered how she could have been ignorant of it so long. The other was sensible that she possessed none of that love to God which the law requires, but could not believe that she entertained such enmity as filled the other with so much remorse and anguish. A few days afterwards, seeing a friend to whom she had expressed this sentiment, she was anxious to let him know her mistake, and informed him she had discovered that she hated God with all her heart.

In the first stages of conviction, it was not easy for the subjects to realize their desert of eternal death. But afterwards, even while they gave decisive evidence of being still as devoid of a right temper as those wretches whose mouths will be stopped by the light of the last day, their conviction of this ill-desert was in many instances very clear. Nevertheless, even to the last, their hearts would recoil at the thought of being in God's hands, and would rise against him for having reserved it to himself to decide whether to sanctify and pardon them or not. Though the display of this doctrine had the most powerful tendency to strip them of all hopes from themselves, and to bring them to the feet of sovereign grace; yet as it thus sapped the foundation on which they rested, their feelings were excited against it. There was a man who, having been well indoctrinated, had for many years advanced this truth, who, notwithstanding, when he came to be concerned about his salvation, and to apply this truth to his own case, was much displeased with it. He was, at times, quite agitated by a warfare between his understanding and his heart; the former assenting to the truth, the latter resisting it. He said it depended on God, and not on himself, whether he ever should comply with the gospel; and for God to withhold his influences, and then punish him for not possessing the temper which these influences alone could produce, appeared to him hard. Before conviction had become deep and powerful, many attempted to exculpate themselves with this plea of inability, and, like their ancestor, to cast the blame upon God, by pleading "The *nature* which *he* gave me, beguiled me." This was the enemy's stronghold. All who were a little more thoughtful than common, but not thoroughly convicted, would, upon the first attack, flee to this refuge. "They would be glad to repent, but *could not*, their *nature* and *heart* were so bad;" as though their nature and heart were not they themselves. But the progress of conviction, in general, soon removed this refuge of lies, and filled them with a sense of utter inexcusableness. And in every case, as soon as their enmity was slain, this plea wholly vanished. Their language immediately became, "I wonder I ever should ask the question, *How can I repent?* My only wonder now is, *that I could hold out so long.*"

It was not uncommon for the hearts of the convicted, as they rose against God, to rise also against his ministers. Several who had not betrayed their feelings in the season of them, afterwards confessed that such resentments had arisen. In some instances the emotions were plainly discoverable; and in one particularly, the subject was so incensed as to break out in bitter expressions but a few hours before being relieved from the anguish of a deeply troubled spirit. Such things seemed to be satisfying evidence that mere conviction no more ameliorates the heart in this, than in the other world; but serves rather to draw out its corruptions into still stronger exercise. It may be suitable to add, that these sallies of resentment were occasioned by the distinguishing doctrines of the gospel closely and affectionately applied to the conscience.

As soon as the heart of stone was taken away, and the heart of flesh given, the subjects of this happy change exhibited sentiments and feelings widely different from those above described. They were now wrapt up in admiration of the laws and absolute government of God, which had been the objects of so much cavil and disgust. Notwithstanding the extreme delicacy and danger which attend the detail of individual cases, it may on the whole, it is hoped, be more useful than injurious to confirm and illustrate the observation just now advanced, by some particular relations.

There was a man who, for a number of years, had entertained a hope of his personal interest in the covenant; and being of inoffensive behavior, had given people no other special ground to distrust him than his opposition to divine sovereignty, and disgust (which he now believes arose from a self-righteous temper,) at the doctrine that God has no regard for the doings of the unregenerate. He thought that the impenitent were thus too much discouraged from making their own exertions. Emboldened by a favorable opinion of his state, he offered himself sometime ago for communion with the church. And because he could not assent to their confession of faith, he petitioned to have several articles struck out, and particularly the one which asserts the doctrine of election. The church did not consent, and he withdrew. But so exquisitely was his sensibility touched, that he had it in serious consideration to dispose of his property, and remove to some place where he might enjoy gospel ordinances. It pleased God, the last winter, to convince him that his feet stood on slippery places; and after a scene of distressing conviction, his mind was composed in view of those very truths which had been the objects of his opposition. Since then, he has publicly manifested his belief in the articles adopted by the church, and has been received by them to the "furtherance" of their "joy of faith," and "comfort of love."

Another might be mentioned who was equally opposed to the essential truths of revelation. Having the care of a school in town the last winter, he was required by the inspectors to subscribe to the belief, that "the *general system* of doctrines taught in the Assembly's Catechism is agreeable to the word of God." He could not comply on the ground that the Catechism asserts, "God hath foreordained whatsoever comes to pass." The inspectors loth to lose him, endeavored to convince him. But this clause appeared to him so exceptionable that he persisted in declining, and would have left the school rather than comply, had he not at last discovered that the phrase *general system* would leave him room after subscribing, to withhold his assent from the offensive article. Soon after this, his conscience was seized by the convincing power of truth. A great revolution was produced in his views and feelings, and he has since professed to be filled with admiration of a government planned by eternal wisdom, and administered by unerring rectitude.

It might, perhaps, not be unsuitable to mention the case of a man upwards of seventy years of age; who, belonging to the lowest class of society, and living in a very retired place, was extremely illiterate, and had little intercourse with the world; yet was possessed of a strong mind and malignant passions. Having conceived a strong disgust at some of the peculiar doctrines of the gospel, he had given his word that he would hear them no more. Because his wife had united with the church, and attended public worship, he rendered her life very uncomfortable. On which subject I went to converse with him last summer; and I am certain I never saw a case in which so much deliberate rancor and deadly hatred were expressed against every thing sacred—against the essential truths of revelation, and against the ministers and church of Christ in general. In the expression both of his countenance and lips, he approximated the nearest to my idea of "the spirits in prison," of any person I ever beheld. His enmity was not awakened to sudden rage, (for my treatment aimed at being conciliatory,) but seemed deep-rooted and implacable. His resolution of keeping from public worship he pertinaciously adhered to; nor had he any connection with the conferences during the first period of the awakening. Yet, disconnected as he was from all religious society and the means of grace, it pleased God late in the winter to take strong hold of his mind. He continued for a while trembling in retirement; but when he could contain no longer, he came out to find the conferences, and to seek some experienced Christians to whom he might lay open his distress. Being called out of town about this time, I did not see him in this condition; and when I saw him he was clothed and in his right mind. Inquiry being made respecting his apprehensions of those doctrines which had been so offensive, he replied, "they are the foundation of the world." Every air seemed changed. Softness and gentleness had taken the place of native ferocity, and the man appeared tamed. I could not help reflecting, that a religion which will make such changes in the tempers and manners of men, is a religion worth possessing. An awakening which produces such effects will not be censured by the friends of human happiness.

It would not consist with the designed brevity of this narration, nor yet, perhaps, with propriety, to detail all the interesting circumstances in the experiences of more than a hundred persons who appear to have been the subjects of this work. It may, however, be useful to go so far into particulars as to exhibit some of the distinguishing fruits of it. The subjects of it have generally expressed a choice that God should pursue the "determinate counsel" of his own will, and without consulting them, decide respecting their salvation. To the question, whether they expected to alter the divine mind by prayer, it has been answered, "I sometimes think, if this were possible I should not dare to pray." When asked what was the first thing which composed their anxious minds, they have sometimes answered, "the thought that I was in the hands of God. It seems to me, that whatever becomes of me, whether I live or die, I cannot bear to be out of his hands." Many have expressed their willingness to put their names to a blank, and leave it with God to fill it up, and *that* because his having the government would secure the termination of all things in his own glory.

They do not found their hopes on the suggestion of Scripture passages to their minds, or dreams, or seeing sights, or hearing voices, or on blind unaccountable impulses; but on the persuasion that they have discovered in themselves the exercises of love to God and man, originating not in selfishness. When asked what they had discovered in God to engage their affections, they have sometimes answered, "I think I love him because he hates sin—because he hates my sins." They have frequently declared that God appeared altogether more glorious to them for being sin-hating and sin-avenging; that they were willing he should abide by his determination not to have mercy on them or their friends, if they would not repent and believe the gospel. One observed in confidence to a friend, and without the appearance of ostentation, that she had been so taken up all day in rejoicing in God's perfections, and the certain accomplishment of his glory, that she had scarcely thought of what would be her own destiny; that she must believe she reckoned more of his glory and the public good than of her own happiness. Some declared that if they could have their choice, either to live a life of religion and poverty, or revel in the pleasures of the world, unmolested by conscience or fear, and at last, be converted on a dying bed, and be as happy hereafter as if they had made the other choice, they should prefer the former; and *that* for the glory of God, and not merely for the happiness which the prospects of future glory would daily afford; for they believed their choice would be the same, though in certain expectation that fears and conflicts would render a religious life less happy than a life of sensuality. Their predominant desire still appears to be that God may be glorified, and that they may render him voluntary glory in a life of obedience, and may enjoy him in a life of communion with him. A prospect of the full attainment of these ends, is what appears to render the heavenly state the object of their eager desire. Their admiration of Jesus Christ seems most excited by his zeal to support his Father's law—a law, the glories of which they appear distinctly though imperfectly to apprehend. The Bible is to them a new book. Prayer seems their delight. Their hearts are peculiarly united to the people of God. But the most observable part of their character, is a lovely appearance of meekness and humility. Little of that presumptuous confidence, too much of which has sometimes appeared in young professors, is observable in them. Accordingly they have not that uninterrupted elevation of spirits which, in the inexperienced, is generally bottomed on comparative ignorance of remaining corruption, and overrating their attainments. Accustomed to discriminate between true and false affections, they appear not to set to their account so much of the "wood, hay, and stubble," as perhaps, some have done. A sense of their ill-desert abides and increases upon them after apparent renovation; a considerable time posterior to which some have been heard to say, "I never had an idea what a heart I had till this week." Each one seems to apprehend his own depravity to be the greatest. They appear not to be calculating to bring God into debt by their new obedience. A person not greatly indoctrinated, but lovely in the charms of child-like simplicity, was heard to say, "I will tell you, sir, what appears to me would be exactly right. It would be exactly right for me to live thirty or forty years in the world without ever sinning again, and be serving God all the time; and then it would be just right for me to be sent to hell for what I have already done." The hopeful subjects of the work as yet exhibit "fruits meet for repentance." Some we have had opportunity to see under the pressure of heavy afflictions, who have seemed calmly to acquiesce in the dispensations of Providence. Many schools have been awakened, and, as we have good reason to conclude, have received lasting benefits. Three of the schools in this town, last winter, were under the care of men professedly pious, and very faithful in imparting religious instruction. Out of these, nearly twenty children in the course of the winter, it is hoped, were introduced into marvelous light. The knowledge possessed by such as we hope have been savingly enlightened by the divine Spirit, is worthy of particular observation. Important ideas and distinctions, which it has been attempted in vain to give to others of their age, appear familiar to them. One lad in particular, in a certain interview which was had with him, discriminated between true and false affections, and stated the grounds of his hope in a manner very surprising. It was the more so, because the evening before an attempt had been made with children of the same age and neighborhood, and of equal abilities and opportunity; and it had seemed like "plowing on a rock," insomuch that the hope was almost relinquished of ever being able to introduce discriminating ideas into minds so young. It would be ungrateful not to acknowledge that in a remarkable manner it hath pleased the Most High "out of the mouths of babes and sucklings to perfect praise."

It is hoped that about fifty heads of families have been the subjects of this work ; a considerable part of whom rank among respectable and influential characters in the town. This, however, gives the young no just encouragement to hazard their salvation on the chance of being called in at the eleventh hour. Had they seen the anguish of some of these for neglecting so long the great business of life, it might discourage such neglect in them. Penetrated with remorse for the waste of life, and for the lax examples by which they supposed they had corrupted others, they seemed to conclude it was probably too late for them to find mercy; yet they were anxious to disburden their conscience of one torment by solemnly warning the youth not to follow their steps. "We are soon going," said they, "to receive the reward of a wasted life ; and we warn you to proceed no further in search of a more convenient time to prepare for death. We have been over the ground between you and us, and this more convenient season does not lie before you. O that we could be placed back to your age, for then we might have hope. If you did but know and feel as we do the value of youth, you would surely better improve it."

In language of this import have they been frequently heard to vent themselves, while despair and anguish seemed settled on every feature; all which united, produced sensations in the affected hearers not easily described.

The power of the Almighty Spirit has prostrated the stoutness of a considerable number, who were the last that human expectation would have fixed on to be the subjects of such a change. One man who lives at a distance from the sanctuary, and who, perhaps, seldom if ever visited it in his life, and who, as might be expected, was extremely ignorant and stupid, has been visited in his own house, and in the view of charity, brought into the kingdom. His heart turns now, for the first time, towards the sanctuary, though ill health prevents him from enjoying the privileges of it. Another old man in the same neighborhood, who had not been in our house of worship, and probably not in any other, for more than twenty years, has been arrested in his retirement by the divine Spirit, and still remains "like the troubled sea when it cannot rest."

It has been a remarkable season for the destruction of false hopes. Nearly twenty of those who have lately appeared to build on the rock, have been plucked off from a sandy foundation. As a caution to others, it may, perhaps, not be improper briefly to state the previous situation of some of these. One had supposed that she loved the God of providence, because she had some sense of his daily kindness to her and her family. She was the one whom I mentioned as having been brought to see that she hated the real character of God with all her heart. Another having been brought up in gay life, was also very ignorant of the essential nature of true religion, insensible of the deceitfulness of her heart, and in full confidence of her good estate. Another, accustomed to contemplate moral truth in the light of a clear and penetrating intellect, had mistaken the assent of the understanding for affections of the heart. Another had been the subject of some exercises in early life, which had induced the hope that he was within the embraces of the gracious covenant. But he had become a worldling, and lived in the neglect of family prayer. Still, while under his late conflicts, he would reach back and fasten anew on his former hope, (which he had made little account of in the days of his carelessness,) until the power of the divine Spirit broke his hold. Another had formerly rested her hope on some suggestion to her mind (somewhat like a voice,) assuring in time of sickness and anxiety, that her sins were forgiven. Another had been introduced into a hoping state in a season of awakening several years ago; since which nothing had occurred as a ground of self-distrust, except that she had sometimes, for a considerable season, neglected prayer and spiritual contemplations for worldly objects. Another was first put upon suspecting and searching himself, by finding in his heart an undue appetite for the gayeties and vanities of youth. He had just returned from a party of pleasure when his conflict began. Another was the man whom I have mentioned as having been so opposed to the sovereignty of God in the dispensations of his grace. The rest, for aught that appeared, were as hopeful candidates for heaven as many professors. From observing the effects which the light of God's presence had upon false hopes, a trembling reflection arose, how many such hopes will be chased away by the opening light of eternity. The Lord seemed to come to "search Jerusalem with candles," and to find out those that were "settled on their lees." The church felt the shock. That same presence which at Sinai made all the church, and even Moses "exceedingly fear and quake," rendered this now a time of trembling with professors in general. Nevertheless, it was with most of them a season of great quickening, and a remarkable day of prayer.

CHAPTER V.

An account of a Revival of Religion in TORRINGTON, CONN., in the years 1798 and 1799. By the Rev. ALEXANDER GILLET.

THE first special appearance of the work among us, was on Wednesday evening, December 26, 1798; on which day two neighboring ministers met at my house agreeably to appointment. After spending some time in prayer and conversation, we had a public lecture, and proposed another for the evening. In the daytime, nothing very remarkable occurred. But in the evening God was visibly present. A discourse was delivered from Proverbs 8: 4, in which were brought into view the nature and importance of true wisdom, and an immediate attention to her voice, interspersed with some pertinent and affecting accounts of the awakening that was prevailing in sundry places. These things were enforced by several addresses. An unusual solemnity filled the place where we were assembled. The friends of Zion present, appeared to receive *a fresh anointing from the Lord,* and to be awakened to a sense of their duty. Some sinners who had labored heretofore under fears about their state, were more deeply and thoroughly impressed, and brought to inquire in earnest, "What must I do to be saved?" And several were first alarmed to view religion as something in which they were highly concerned. Thus the important scene opened, which has been truly wonderful, and expressive of divine power and grace. It was found to be the case, however, that there had been something unusual on the minds of a number previous to this remarkable meeting. They had not felt easy for some time. Still this was the first sensible exhibition of the work.

The appearance and the effects gradually increased from that time to May and June ensuing. The minds of one and another were impressed, especially among the youth, till they in general became thoughtful. A goodly number, we charitably hope, were made the subjects of the convicting and transforming operations of the Spirit of God. Some in the more advanced stages of life have experienced the same gracious influences. For a season, a general seriousness appeared to pervade the society. These favorable appearances were very promising in June; when, towards the close of that month, a fatal bar was thrown in the way, by some hasty sectarian disputes. After they subsided, and the work appeared to revive again, the attention did not recover its former aspect. It has rather decreased from that unhappy period.

The number that have come forward and made a profession of religion, is forty-five, including several who obtained hope before the commencement of this revival. Among this number there are twenty young persons from fourteen years and upwards, nine males and eleven females. The proportion of the whole number is, seventeen males, and twenty-eight females. There are, besides, upwards of thirty who have expressed a hope that they are the subjects of this wonderful work; but have not as yet dared to come forward, because they fear that they have been deceived.

It was wonderful to see what pains persons took, for a season, to attend lectures and conferences. When a meeting was appointed, they would go through storm, cold, and bad roads to attend. And when they had been attending for two or three hours, they were so far from being wearied, that it was with difficulty they could be persuaded to retire. It was not uncommon to have a full meeting, though the weather was stormy and exceedingly forbidding. "This is the Lord's doing, and it is marvelous in our eyes."

The impression was so great and extensive, and the work so *new* and *unusual*, that for a time the adversary was confounded. Those who were willing to oppose, had their mouths shut for months, and stood gazing and wondering. And what increased this confusion among gainsayers, was, the method Providence took to carry on his gracious operations, different from what had been usual in former awakenings. There had been complaints heretofore, of irregularities and enthusiasm. But this work was marked with the *still small voice*. Those under serious convictions appeared steady in attending to the things of religion. When they obtained comfort, it did not seem to arise from mere impressions on the imagination, but from such a view of God and divine things as they never before experienced. The lectures and conferences too, have been conducted with great regularity. Persons have appeared far from discovering a spirit of self-importance, and forwardness to lead in meetings. The general characteristic has been, a wish for instruction and direction.

When the mind was arrested, the sinner trembled. At first, he did not see that he merited such dreadful treatment at the hand of God as everlasting burnings. The thought was overwhelming. True, he could not deny his sins; but he would think he was not so bad as some represented—that his heart was not so opposed to his Maker, and so unwilling to be reconciled to him. On seriously attending to his case, he was soon made apprehensive of his mistake. By reading, instructions, counsels and warnings, he was brought under convictions, that the Scripture God is the true God, the creator and great sovereign of the universe—that the law is just and holy, and of the most serious nature—that he had violated this law, and become exposed to its insupportable curse—that his heart was far more sinful and stubborn than he had imagined—that he was in the hand of this God, and could not escape—and that he had no assurance of his life. The more he became acquainted with the Scriptures and himself, the clearer these truths appeared to him; especially the poisonous nature of his heart, its pride, unwillingness to bow before God, and murmuring at the conditions of life. His anxiety and foreboding apprehensions rose in proportion to these views. He was finally brought to see himself in the hand of God, justly condemned, and the object of his mere sovereign mercy. The Lord must save him.

Mercy was all his hope. The degree of light and conviction varied in different persons; but this is the general description of it. They were evidently slain by the law before they were made alive by Jesus Christ. Before relief came, they were reduced to a condition sensibly helpless and disconsolate, apprehending nothing but endless misery. And when this load of distress was removed, it was done in a way, and at a time, which they did not expect. The prophet Isaiah gives a just view of their case in these affecting words—" And I will bring the blind by a way they know not, I will lead them in paths they have not known. I will make darkness light before them, and crooked things straight." Isaiah 42 : 16.

Previous to the new birth, the subjects of the work have had clear convictions of the native depravity of their hearts. They have commonly found them seats of pride, selfishness, and awful stubbornness. They have been led to think, that the fountain within them was worse than in others, that their hearts were more hardened, more deceitful, and unmanageable. Some have been sensible of such shocking feelings as these—" O, how I wish there was no God, heaven nor hell. I had rather be like the beasts that perish, than be in the hand of such a God as this!" After they had experienced the great change, they appeared to themselves far worse than before. Then they could exclaim, "I thought I knew something of my heart before, but I knew nothing of it. It appears to me a sink of all treachery, corruptions and abominations! How can I be a Christian? Can I be a new creature, and have my heart filled with so many vain thoughts, and strange imaginations?" The hopeful converts all agree that the heart of the Christian is very different from what they had imagined. So is his life. They had expected to be almost free from the influence of sinful propensities—to have grown better and better—and to have made great progress in godliness. This flattering notion was soon changed by experience. The appearance to them has been, that they grow more deficient and vile before God.

Another conspicuous feature of the work is, that when God had taken off their distressful burden, they, at first, had no suspicions of their hearts being renewed. They were rather alarmed with the apprehension that the Spirit of God had forsaken them. They trembled in view of returning to a state of carnal and dreadful security, and becoming more hardened than ever. They were ready to cry out, "I wish I could feel as concerned for myself as I have done; but I cannot. What will become of me now!" While in this situation, they have been asked, how the character of God appeared? They readily answered, "Great, excellent, glorious! I wish for no other God to govern the world. There is none like him. I can't wish for any other Saviour besides Christ—nor any other way to be saved, but that of the gospel. All seems right. God is such a glorious being, that methinks I could praise him, even if he should cast me off." This frame has sometimes continued for several days before they dared to hope. They wondered what had become of their burden. In time, however, experience taught them that this anxious load was taken off in consequence of the heart's being made to love that very God and religion, which before, they had been hating and opposing. Now they stood astonished, that they had never seen these things before.

The doctrines made use of in carrying on this work, is another distinguishing feature of it. These are the soul-humbling doctrines of our Saviour, which exalt God, and stain all the pride of human glory. The divine sovereignty—the holiness, extent and inflexibility of the moral law—human depravity—our entire dependence on God—the special agency of the Holy Spirit in conviction and conversion—and mere grace through Jesus Christ as the Mediator;—these have been kept constantly in view, more or less, and proved like a fire and hammer that breaketh the flinty rock in pieces.

It has been common for awakened sinners to think hard of the decrees of God, election, and unconditional submission, and to struggle for a while against them. But they were finally brought to a thorough conviction that these doctrines which were so terrible to them, were their only hope. Their contest ceased, and the divine sovereignty and its kindred doctrines, became their peculiar joy and support. In close connection with what has now been said, it was remarked, that the most plain, pungent preaching has been accompanied with far the greatest success.

Finally—As to the abiding effects of the work, the hopeful converts appear to exhibit a real change of character. There has, as yet, been no instance of apostacy among those who have professed religion. Among a number of others who *hope*, with whom I have particularly conversed, there has been none in my acquaintance. This is all of God, and a practical demonstration of the truth of the gospel which unbelievers so foolishly despise. We live in a wonderful day. We fear, and rejoice with trembling. May Zion prosper, and all the kind, benevolent purposes of God be accomplished.

CHAPTER VI.

An account of a Revival of Religion in Plymouth, Conn., in the year 1799. By Rev. Samuel Waterman.

Towards the end of the year 1798, there was an appearance of more attention to religion than had been common among us, although it was not noticed at the time. Our assemblies on the Sabbath were more full, and the attention of the congregation to the Word preached, and other parts of social worship, more fixed than had been usual. Nothing farther very specially appeared, until the month of February, 1799, when the Spirit came like a mighty rushing wind, and seemed to breathe on many at one and the same time. The first visible indication of this, was on a lecture day, previous to the sacramental supper. These lectures had heretofore usually been attended but by few, besides professors, and too many of these were negligent in their attendance. But at this time there were, probably, three, if not four times the number which had ordinarily attended on such occasions, especially of the young people, and the countenances of many indicated sadness of heart. Indeed the whole congregation appeared solemn; but some in different parts of the house, by their tears which they could not conceal, manifested that their minds were tenderly impressed. At the close of this meeting in the daytime, an evening lecture was appointed, which, it is believed, was the first evening religious meeting which had ever been publicly notified, or attended, in the town. At this meeting, a much greater number attended than in the daytime. A brother in the ministry being present, preached from these words—" He flattereth himself in his own eyes, until his iniquity be found to be hateful." The assembly was solemn, the hearers attentive, and the Word preached seemed to be accompanied with divine power. A religious meeting was now appointed on the Wednesday evening of the next week; and although the season, and the traveling, were both uncomfortable, many came from almost every quarter; and it seemed as if God was present of a truth, speaking to sinners in a still small voice, and saying what have you been doing? And where are you going? Consider what you do, and what your end is like to be. After praying and singing, the people were addressed from these words—" Escape for thy life ; look not behind thee ; neither stay thou in all the plain ; escape to the mountain, lest thou be consumed." A solemn silence reigned among the hearers, who appeared to hear as for their lives ; and many were to be seen in various parts of the house, weeping and trembling under a sense of their guilt and danger ; and saying to themselves, " What must I do to be saved?" For at this time, but few spake out the feelings and exercises of their hearts ; but at the close of the meeting, they returned to their homes, in pensive sadness. From that time to the present, there have been almost every week from two to five, and sometimes six religious meetings, beside the two upon the Sabbath ; as I have invariably attended them myself, I can witness to the order and decency, the silence and solemnity, with which, and the numbers by which, these meetings have been attended. The silence observed among those who were going to, or returning from these meetings, was very impressive, and frequently noticed with surprise and pleasure. Little or no tumult or noise, and the appearance of most, much as if they had been going to, or were returning from the funeral of some near relative or friend. And while in the house, nothing was said but by the minister; for so little disposed were the people to take an active part in any religious exercise, except singing, that it was difficult to get one publicly to propose or ask a question. Many were swift to hear, but all slow to speak.

In this time of God's pouring out of his Spirit and reviving his work among us, sixty-one have been added to the church, and baptism administered to about one hundred. Among the baptized are sixteen households or families. At one time, a number of households, containing about twenty souls, were baptized.

Those who have, in this time of awakening, joined the church, are most, if not all of them, between fourteen and forty years of age. The greatest number have been from the class of married people. Of the unmarried, twenty-one are females.

I shall now give some further particulars relating to this revival of religion.

About four or five months after the attention began, two lads or young men, who lived near each other, having finished their daily labor in the field, met in a school-house near by, and spent the evening in religious conversation. They had not spent more than two evenings in this manner, before their being together, and the design thereof, was known to some in the neighborhood, who, the next time they met, joined their company. About this time I heard of their meeting, although it was not generally known. A doubt, at once, arose with respect to the propriety of encouraging so young a class, of the different sexes, meeting by themselves, for religious purposes, without some one of more age and experience, to superintend their meetings, and preserve regularity among them, as also to instruct them in things pertaining to the kingdom of God, and their own salvation. At their next meeting, I went among them, and found nearly forty males and females, from about eight to eighteen years of age, convened for the purpose of praying together, reading, singing psalms, and talking upon religious subjects. Being now desired by them, I met with them weekly for several months. The second time I met with them, there were about double the number there were the first time; and the third time, there were, I judged, about one hundred and forty. Although it was now the busiest season of the year with farmers, being about harvest time, and the evenings short, young men and women and children came from a distance of several miles; and much the greatest part appeared to have their minds impressed with seriousness; for in every part of the house, tears were seen, and sighs and sobs heard; although endeavors were used to suppress the one, and to conceal the other. These meetings of young people and children were kept up for several months, and until more elderly people, who wished to participate with them in their devotional exercises, came in among them, and so rendered them common for those of every age. But it is hoped that the religious impressions made, at this time, upon the young and tender minds of a number, will never be wholly effaced, but will remain through time, and be like a well of water, springing up into everlasting life.

I shall now take notice of some expressions, or forms of speech, made use of by individuals, during the time of the awakening. These expressions and forms of speech, so far as they indicate the exercises of the heart, will show what the views and feelings of some were; and perhaps afford a specimen of the whole; for it is not doubted that similar views and feelings were common to many, if not to most of those among us, who have been the subjects of an uncommon operation of the Spirit.

When one was asked, "Do you hope you have acquainted yourself with God, and are now at peace with him? or should you leave the world this night, what would your end be?" the answer was, "I do not know what my state is, nor what will become of me. I am in the hands of God, who has a right to do, and who will do as he pleases, and I know he will do right." Question. "Do you think yourself a sinner, and that you deserve to be forever separated from God, and to be made everlastingly miserable?" Answer. "Yes, I know I am a sinner, and deserve eternal death; and if God should cast me off forever, and make me everlastingly miserable, I should never have any just cause to complain." Question. "Do you feel reconciled to the will of God? Is it the joy of your heart that the Lord reigns; and can you trust yourself in his hands, and leave it with him to do with you as he pleases?" Answer. "It seems to me, I can. I know he does, and will do right." Question. "Do you think you love God for what he is in himself?" Answer. "I hope I do." Question. "If God should reject and cast you off forever, do you think you should still love him?" Answer. "I should have the same reason to love him for what he is in himself, as I should if he should make me happy, and it seems to me that I should love him then, as much as I now do." Question. "Do you feel willing to be eternally separated from God, and banished his presence forever?" Answer. "No, I do not. But if I should be, God would still be a just and good being, for I deserve his wrath forever."

To another it was said, "When I asked you a few months ago, what you thought would become of you if you was then to die, you told me, you hoped it would be well with you; but you did not at that time give the reason of your hope. What do you think of yourself now?" "I think, sir, if I had died when you spoke to me before, I should have been in misery now; for I then deceived myself; but I hope I am not deceived now, and think, if I should leave the world at this time, I should go to rest." "But you say you have been deceived, and what reason have you to believe that your present hope is not that of the hypocrite, which will fail when God shall take away the soul?" Answer. "I have views and feelings now which I never had before. I never had such views of God and Christ, as I now do." Question.

"Are you so confident of your good estate, as that you are not afraid to die?" Answer. "Sometimes I am, and sometimes I am not. Sometimes I feel as if I wished I was dead." Question. "Do you ever feel a willingness to leave your relations, and companions and friends, and now in the days of your youth, lie down in the cold and silent grave?" Answer. "Yes, sometimes I do." Question. "But why do you not feel so at all times?" Answer. "Sometimes I am afraid I do not love Christ in sincerity, and then I am afraid to die; but at other times, I have such views of Christ, and he appears so glorious and lovely, that I have a desire to be gone, that I might be with him, and love him more, and serve him better than I do, or can do, while I live in this world."

To another, who expressed a desire to profess Christ and commune at his table, it was said, "Do you think yourself worthy to come to the table of the Lord?" The answer was, "No, I know I am not; but the dogs eat of the crumbs that fall from their master's table, and this, sir, is what I wish to be permitted to do. I think it my duty to confess Christ before men, and unworthy as I am, I have a desire to commune with him at his table." Question. "Do you feel a love for holiness, a hungering and thirsting after righteousness, a relish for, and delight in the duties of religion?" Answer. "Yes, above any thing in the world. I used to think I took pleasure in being in young company, in attending balls and other amusements; but I now take more satisfaction in reading the Bible, conversing upon religion and attending to religious duties, than in any thing else; and I have more comfort in attending one religious meeting, than I ever took in all the balls I ever attended. And although I have read the Bible through several times, I never open it now, but I find something new in it—something I never saw before."

To another it was said, "Do you find by experience that Christ's yoke is easy, and his burden light; his ways pleasant, and his paths peace?" Answer. "Yes, and I now believe there is no real happiness in any other way than walking with God, and keeping his commandments. I have lived a number of years in the world, without God, and without attending to the duties of religion, and then thought myself happy; but I never knew what happiness was, until of late. I have enjoyed more real happiness within a few months, or even weeks, than I ever enjoyed in all my life before."

Another said, "I never till of late, knew

what friendship meant. I never loved and enjoyed my friends and acquaintance as I now do. I wish to do them all the good I can, and I want they should experience the power of godliness, and taste and see how good the Lord is. I lately attended public worship upon the Sabbath, in a neighboring town. The minister preached a very serious and good sermon, and appeared to feel the importance of what he said; but many of the hearers, especially of the young people, were very inattentive, and some of them very rude. O, how did I wish some word spoken by the preacher, might reach their consciences, and some arrow prick their hearts, check their levity and make them serious. To see a minister spending his strength for nought, and young people trifling and playing in the house of God, gave me very disagreeable feelings; and if my heart does not deceive me, I wish all may be saved."

Another said, "In early life I was thoughtful about religion, and for many years past, had a great desire to profess Christ, and commune at his table. But doubts and fears respecting my preparedness for transactions so solemn and important, always kept me back, until of late, when my mind hath been so strongly impressed with a sense of its being my duty, I could refrain no longer. I therefore publicly gave up myself to God, and the same day communed at the Lord's table; but not without fear and trembling lest I should eat and drink unworthily. The night following, as I lay in bed, meditating upon what I had done, examining myself, and praying to God that he would lead me in the way everlasting, I suddenly had such manifestations of God and Christ, and such a time of refreshing, as I never had before. It seemed as if I beheld heaven opened, and Christ standing on the right hand of God. Not that I saw any thing with my bodily eyes. The whole was mental. God appeared glorious in holiness, and as an absolute sovereign, and Christ an able and willing Saviour. My heart appeared at once reconciled to God, and I seemed to have no choice of my own; but my will seemed to be swallowed up in his will. Christ appeared both able and willing to save me, unworthy as I was. I now experienced such joy as I never did before. I attempted to describe it to a friend in bed with me; but it was joy unspeakably great—joy unutterable. My whole soul seemed to be swallowed up in viewing God and Christ, without reflecting that I had, or ever should have any interest in either of them. I rejoiced in God, and rejoiced in Christ, on account of the glorious beauty and excellencies which I saw in them. From that moment, I have felt a sweet calmness and serenity of mind. I seem to have no will of my own, but my will bowed to the will of God in life and death, for time and for eternity. I feel as if I could leave myself and all that I have, with God, for him to do with me and them as he thinks best; being fully assured that he will do right. If I am finally saved, it will be of his sovereign mercy and grace, through the atonement of Christ; and if I am finally lost, God will be just and good, and the faulty cause of my perdition will lie at my own door. This Lord's day night, and the ravishing views I then had, I shall never forget; and my daily prayer is, that I may have times of refreshing from the presence of the Lord; and that I may be more conformed in God in the temper of my mind, and have more of the spirit of Christ."

Another said, "As I was walking to the house of God upon the Sabbath, I saw a number of little worms, swimming about in a small brook. I stopped and viewed them, and said to myself, how innocent and happy are these worms, compared with such a sinful wretch as I am. They never dishonored the God that made them, as I have done. They never slighted the

Saviour, nor grieved the holy Spirit of God as I have done. They never committed the sins that I have committed. O, how mean and vile I am! I am meaner and viler than the meanest and most contemptible worm. How wonderful and astonishing that God should suffer such an unworthy, ill-deserving creature as I am to live in his world, to tread upon his earth, or to breathe his air. I deserved to have been shut up in hell long ago, and yet I am still a prisoner of hope. O, the goodness and long-suffering of God, and the ingratitude and wickedness of hardened sinners!"

I shall now subjoin a few extracts from some letters sent to particular friends. They were not written with a view of being seen by any but the persons to whom they were addressed. One writes thus:

"Dear Friend—The spring is now opening, the snow dissolving, the streams murmuring over the pebbles, the lambs skipping in the meadows, and the birds on the branches straining their little throats in melodious songs. All speak, in different ways, their Maker's praise. Should not we, who are endowed with reason, join in praising the Creator, even the mute creation would find a voice, and upbraid our silence. Let us in our youth attend to the one thing needful. Now is the best time to lay in store a good foundation against the time to come. It is written, 'Remember now thy Creator in the days of thy youth.' And now is the accepted time. If you ask what this world is, and what its pleasures are? I answer, vanity of vanities, all is vanity. There is no real and substantial happiness in the enjoyment of any thing which this world affords. If your ideas of this world are the same with mine, then

> 'Whilst the busy crowd,
> The vain, the wealthy, and the proud,
> In folly's maze advance,
>   Though singularity and pride
> Be called our lot,
>   We'll step aside,
> Nor join the giddy dance.'"

The same writes again:

"I retire from company to converse alone with one whom I love; for so I call writing to a friend. What privileges have we, of which thousands are deprived. We have kind parents to instruct us—we are taught to write, and thus to converse with absent friends. Let us improve our advantages, and cultivate our minds in early life. Doing this will render us dutiful children and faithful friends; render

PLYMOUTH, CONN. 107

the path through life pleasing, and a death-bed easy. When I hear people complaining of their misfortunes, and hardships, I often say in my heart, alas, there is no cause of complaint, but the highest reason for gratitude and praise. Nature is eloquent in praising the Creator,

> But man alone intent to stray,
> Ever turns from wisdom's way.

Until you see me, do think of me, or think of something better. Adieu."

Another writes thus:

"Dear Friend—I now sit down to tell you what has taken place with me this present week. On Wednesday evening, I was thoughtful and very serious, and after attentively listening to some religious conversation between two friends, I retired to rest, with my mind deeply impressed, and lay sometime in bed, wetting my pillow with tears. This was not the first time my mind has been fixed on, and my thoughts swallowed up with things of another world; and I have sometimes entertained a hope that I experienced the power of godliness in my childhood. But now on a sudden, my sins were set in order before me, and seemed to stare me in the face; and my heart was so pricked that I could not lie still. I used to think I had a desire to embrace Christ, and partake of gospel blessings. But I now experienced views and feelings, such as I never did before, and was afraid to close my eyes in sleep; for I thought nothing kept me from the pit of endless perdition, but the slender and brittle thread of life. What shall I do? was now the language of my heart. If the righteous are scarcely saved, where shall the ungodly and the sinner appear? If I attempted to pray, these words were in my mind, the prayer of the wicked is abomination to the Lord. I then said to myself, what can I, or what shall I do? I am wretched, and wretched I must be. I deserve nothing but the frowns and wrath of the Almighty. Better would it have been for me, if I had not been born. At this time, my views, exercises and feelings were such as I cannot express. They were such as I never had before. But at this moment, my heart breathed out the prayer of the publican, who thought himself unworthy to lift up so much as his eyes to heaven, 'God be merciful to me a sinner.' Immediately upon this, I appeared to myself to be lost, for a short space. I believe it was not more than a minute or two, but I do not know how long it was, nor what passed during the time, for whether I was in the body, or out, I cannot tell. But as soon as I came to myself, I did from my heart give up myself, both soul and body, to Him who gave me my being. After I had thus given myself up to God, being much fatigued, and having had but very little sleep since Monday night, I fell asleep; and when I awoke, found my mind more at ease than it was before. But I seemed to myself to be a new creature. I could not tell how I was altered, but I thought, surely I am not the same person I used to be. In the forenoon of Thursday, while I was about my common domestic concerns, many tears fell from my eyes, not because I was concerned about the salvation of my own soul; but O, the goodness of God! In the afternoon, I attended the sacramental lecture, and heard a sermon from these words—' Jesus, when he had cried again with a loud voice, yielded up the ghost.' The words of the text affected my heart, and the sermon seemed to do my soul good. He died for sinners. Happy are those that trust in him. In the evening, I attended a religious meeting, and what I heard was to me as cold water to a thirsty soul. During most of the day, I had by turns, doubts and fears respecting my future state. But at night, I felt as if I could trust myself in the hands of God, and having committed myself to his keeping, I gave myself to sleep, saying, I will both lay me down in peace, and sleep, for thou Lord makest me to dwell in safety. I spent most of the forenoon of Friday in reading and writing, and in the afternoon I began to entertain a hope that I had seen, and been with Jesus, who hath said, they that seek me early, shall find me. To-day, namely, Saturday, my hope is strong; and I believe if God ever did pour his Spirit into my heart, he did it last Wednesday evening. But at that time, I thought of no such thing. My prayer now is, that God, for Jesus' sake, would pour out his spirit upon all flesh."

During the time that the awakening continued, sports and pastimes, and ceremonious visits were generally discontinued; and the ball-room was so far unoccupied, that the musician found that his craft was in danger, and that his hopes of gain were gone. And in those days, the Word of the Lord, both read and preached, was precious. To many, the Bible appeared to be a new book.

Although much time was spent in religious exercises, such as reading, attending lectures, and other religious meetings, yet in such a manner did those who were serious economize, and redeem time, that it was believed by unbiased and candid observers, that worldly business did not suffer by means of the religious attention.

A good number of families who had always lived without calling upon God either morning or evening, are now devout worshipers.

To see, or hear of such revivals of religion, and times of reformation, must refresh and gladden the hearts of all the godly, and excite the children of Zion, while they rejoice in their king, and in the prosperity of his kingdom, to pray without ceasing, that he would hasten the time, even the set time for the accomplishment of all those glorious things spoken of in prophecy, concerning the enlargement, peace, prosperity and glory of Christianity. When the enemy shall come in like a flood, the Spirit of the Lord shall lift up a standard against him; but for this he will be inquired of by the house of Israel. And with what freedom and importunity, may God's spiritual Israel address the throne of grace for so rich a blessing. Did he ever say to the seed of Jacob, Seek ye me in vain?

> "He frees the souls condemned to death,
> And when his saints complain,

> It shan't be said that praying breath
> Was ever spent in vain."

He that shall come, saith, behold I come quickly. Amen. Even so come, Lord Jesus.

CHAPTER VII.

An account of a Revival of Religion in GRANVILLE, MASS., in the years 1798 and 1799. By the REV. TIMOTHY M. COOLEY.

For a few months previous to the late revival, it was a time of very great stupidity. The wise and the foolish slumbered together. Our youth had become much addicted to sinful diversions. In one of their scenes of amusement, God was pleased to frown upon them in a very awful manner. While they were engaged in their thoughtless recreations, two young men were seized violently ill, and carried out of the ball-chamber. A young woman, in consequence of a cold which she took on the same evening, was in a very short time taken with a fever and delirium, and brought to the brink of the grave. She afterwards recovered, and became a hopeful subject of divine grace. One of the young men before mentioned, after a short illness died. This unhappy youth being told by his weeping mother that he was dying, replied with his expiring breath, "O, I cannot die. I am unprepared." These alarming dispensations of divine Providence, rendered the minds of the young people solemn, and gave a check to their sinful pleasures. Many were then convinced of the danger and criminality of those amusements, which they once esteemed innocent.

In the Spring of the year 1798, professors were much awakened, and ardently desired a revival of religion. Christian parents were anxious for their children; and it was common to hear pious people in conversation, breathing out their earnest desires for the effusions of the Spirit. There was a visible engagedness among professors, and many, like Simeon of old, were "waiting for the consolation of Israel."

I invited a number of the youth into my study, and urged upon them the necessity of the one thing needful. This was a very solemn meeting, and will, probably, be long remembered by some who were present.

On the second Sabbath in June, a very plain sermon was preached from Ezekiel, 37 : 3, which was blessed to the awakening of a number of secure sinners. In the evening, a conference was attended which exhibited evident marks of unusual seriousness. The next Sabbath evening a conference was attended, and many appeared to feel the weight of truth at heart. The next Tuesday a number of young people met for a civil visit, and the violin was introduced, which, instead of producing the usual hilarity, occasioned a flood of tears. The work of the Spirit, which had been for several days concealed, now burst forth. It could be no longer concealed. It was found that numbers had, for some time, felt a very serious concern for their future well-being, and thought they were alone in it, being ignorant of the feelings and resolutions of others. Two young persons, who had been very active in the follies of youth, mutually agreed to begin a new life, little suspecting that a number of their companions had secretly formed the same resolution. The glorious work spread with surprising rapidity through the parish. There was suddenly a noise among the dry bones. Christians were animated—sinners were awakened—and scoffers were struck silent at the powerful work of the Almighty. There were but very few, whether old or young, who did not experience some serious alarms. It was truly a remarkable season with us, and the most aged had never witnessed the like before. I shall give the reader an imperfect idea of that surprising change, from apparent thoughtlessness to universal alarm, which took place within two or three weeks. Those who were not at first truly converted, were made solemn by what they saw in others, and afterwards became the subjects of genuine conversion.

The next Sabbath, the assembly appeared almost as solemn as if that day were to close their earthly existence. The assembly, though crowded, was almost as still as the burying ground. Our meetings were distinguished for a still, solemn, listening attention to the Word; and the audience hung upon the lips of the speaker as if they realized that their all for eternity was at stake.

The rapidity of the work must be ascribed primarily to the all-conquering influences of the Holy Spirit. But it is worthy of notice, that most of the inhabitants of this place are descendants of five or six families. There is, consequently, a great degree of friendship and intimacy among them, and a striking similarity in their feelings, manners and sentiments. Those who were first impressed, communicated their feelings and resolutions to their relatives of a similar age, and urged them to join with them in living a new life. These private warnings were a means of spreading the work.

Their views and feelings while under conviction, were as follows:

They encouraged themselves, that, by a few weeks' seriousness and diligence in duties, they should prepare themselves for regeneration. After persevering awhile in these external duties, they thought their prayers and cries had been sufficient to prevail with God to show mercy. They secretly found fault with God for withholding his grace. The heart rose against divine sovereignty. Some thought hard of God for giving comfort to others, while he denied it to them. The enmity of the heart rose up, like a venomous serpent, against the Almighty. Such exercises as these, discovered to them the total depravity of their hearts. They felt convinced, that the garment of self-righteousness, which was so pleasing to them, covered a heart full of opposition to God's character. They were before convinced that they had been guilty of many outward acts of sin, but now they saw something of the fountain of pollution within. They were convinced that they had never prayed, read, or cried, as God required. They still persevered in duties, but seemed, as they expressed it, to grow worse and worse. They discovered that God's law justly condemned them, and that they must be rescued by sovereign mercy, or suffer its awful sanction.

The views and exercises of those who obtained a hope, were as follows:

There was a great diversity as to the manner in which divine light was let into the mind, and at the same time, a wonderful similarity in their feelings after the admission of true light. Some obtained relief by a view of the glory and excellency of Christ. He appeared to be the chiefest among ten thousand, and altogether lovely. Others were led to see the excellency of the Gospel plan, and its fitness for sinners. Others felt a happy and joyful submission to God as a sovereign, and were willing to be entirely in his hands. When God's time had come to show mercy, their opposition was subdued. They felt willing to be wholly in the hands of that God who hath mercy on whom he will have mercy. They had new views of God, of the Saviour, of the Bible, and of Christian people. Old things had passed away, behold all things had become new. They felt a sweet calmness of mind, but in most instances, had not a thought at the time of it, that what they experienced was regeneration. It was sometimes several days before they dared to hope they were new creatures. They rejoiced with fear. In many instances, a hope was obtained and gradually confirmed, by comparing themselves with the Word, and finding a degree of that submission and disinterested love which characterize those who are born again.

The work of the Spirit in this place has been remarkably free from enthusiasm and confusion. There have been no instances of very great distress or outcries under convictions, nor of enthusiastic rants of joy, after receiving comfort. The work was mild.

This revival of religion has been productive of these happy effects. The Bible has been studied—family prayer revived—the instruction of children promoted—the sanctuary crowded—and the distinguishing doctrines of the gospel more thoroughly studied and understood. Zion's God has discovered his sovereignty as well as his mercy among us. Some of the most gay and thoughtless have become hopeful converts, whilst others, who were more sober and moral, were passed by. Some have been hopefully new-born who were educated in irreligious, prayerless families, while others were passed by who enjoyed a pious education. But it must be confessed, that those who had been religiously educated, were more generally the subjects of special grace.

Within one year after the beginning of the awakening, upwards of fifty united with the church. Others have been since added. And about twenty more, mostly young people, have obtained a hope in this season of refreshing, and by a sober life, they give evidence of a real change; but through prevailing doubts and diffidence, have not dared to make a public profession.

In some instances, almost whole families fled to the ark of safety. In one family, I found seven or eight, and in others five or six, who thought they could rejoice in God. We had the pleasing sight of four sisters offering themselves to receive Christian baptism and unite with the church.

It is now above three years since the beginning of this glorious work, and I can give a more ample testimony to its genuineness, than I could have done in months that are past. "By their fruits ye shall know them." Many who received slight impressions, have become like the seed which fell on stony places. And to some who entertained a hope that they were renewed, "it hath happened according to the true proverb." 2 Pet. 2: 22. And with great concern we may conclude, that "their last state is worse than the first," seeing they crucify unto themselves the Son of God afresh, and put him to open shame.

But those who have made a profession of religion, and a number of others who have not professed publicly, appear to be steadfast and unmovable; and their conversation is in a good measure agreeable to the gospel. There may be tares among the wheat. "And let him that thinketh he standeth, take heed lest he fall." Nearly one half who have lately become professors are in youth. They have cheerfully relinquished their former sinful amusements; and have often declared, that they have enjoyed more real happiness in one religious meeting than in all their past follies and sinful mirth. They, in general, appear to be ornaments to their profession, and by their presence at our sacramental table, render the communion a very delightful duty.

"The Lord hath done great things for us, whereof we are glad." The repentance of a number of Christless sinners in this place, has doubtless given joy to angels and saints above. And we trust that a goodly number will praise God to eternity, for what they have experienced in this revival of religion. "The Lord hath brought them up out of the horrible pit, out of the miry clay, and set their feet upon a rock; and he hath put a new song into their mouth, even praise to the living God."

CHAPTER VIII.

An account of a Revival of Religion in HARWINTON, CONN., in the year 1799. By the Rev. JOSHUA WILLIAMS.

In the latter part of January and beginning of February, 1799, our meetings for public worship were very full, and more solemn than I had ever seen upon any occasion before. In the second week of February, I attended several meetings in neighboring societies, in company with a number of ministers. The Lord appeared to be present in a remarkable manner. On Friday I returned home, with two or three of my brethren. A lecture had been previously appointed. The congregation was very large, and the effects of the Word were very visible. In the evening, another sermon was preached, and some exhortations given. The effects were still more visible. It is believed that on this, and the two succeeding days, more than a hundred persons received deep impressions of their miserable state; and many of them were feelingly convicted of their total depravity of heart, and absolute helplessness. In the two following weeks, the solemnity, concern and conviction evidently increased. Many were brought to see that a selfish religion, such as theirs was, was unsafe; and that they must have a principle, higher than the fear of hell or desire of happiness, to prompt them in the path of life. It is not in my power to describe the anxiety which appeared in many. They found themselves transgressors in every thing. The more they saw of themselves, the more they were convinced of their desert of endless misery. This again increased their anxiety, so that in a general way, sleep almost fled from their eyes, and when they went about the necessary concerns of life, their spirits were loaded with sorrow and distress.

This anxiety continued with some longer than with others, before they found relief. A conviction of their selfish regards in all their attempts to pray, led them to reflect that their prayer was sin. It added to their apprehensions that God might refuse to hear. A holy, sin-hating sovereign might strike them dead in the attempt. And to refrain from prayer was still more dangerous. Danger appeared on all sides, and *What must I do?* was a constant and earnest inquiry. At this time, the importance of divine truth was so generally fixed upon the mind, that I could scarcely go into a house without discovering evidences of great attention to the Bible. It was read with earnestness as the word of life.

Some were wrought upon very suddenly, and in such circumstances as made it evident that it was not of themselves, or of any man, but of God. From the 14th to the 20th of April, there were eighteen instances of hopeful conversion. Several were brought under sorrowful and distressing conviction at midnight, on their beds—and many in such circumstances that it could not be accounted for on any principle, but the sovereign power and mercy of God. At this time, the labor of preaching was easy indeed; but to detect the false hope to which many were prone, like drowning men, who catch hold of any thing that comes in their way, was a difficult and critical business. Never did I feel the importance of the ministry, and my own insufficiency, so much as at this period. On the one hand, not to wound the lambs of Christ's flock, and on the other, not to encourage the unfounded hope of the self-deceiver, required the utmost caution and diligence. My usual practice was, if upon examination, I found marks of a false hope, to tell the matter plainly. But if there were symptoms of a well-founded hope, I told them that they must prove their hope to be genuine by their future holy conduct, always remembering that the heart is deceitful above all things.

In the month of May, four were added to the church—in July, fifty-six were added in one day, the solemnities of which were blest to the awakening of some others. In September, twenty-four more were added, and several others at different times, making the whole number one hundred; several more, it is probable, will soon join with them. The whole number for whom I have entertained a hope of their real regeneration, is more than a hundred; and though with grief, I must say that a few do not appear to hold out, yet the perseverance of the others, especially of those who have made a profession, bids me still hope that the greatest part will continue steadfast to the end. Many of them have obtained a precious degree of knowledge and love, and appear to be growing in the graces of the Christian.

I now proceed to mention some particular cases.

One instance is that of a woman who died with the small pox, about twenty-five years of age. From her younger years, she was a woman of uncommon candor, prudence and gentleness; nor was she entirely destitute of thoughts on serious subjects. By many of her acquaintances, she was thought to be prepared for heaven years ago. But she totally disclaimed such an idea. She was a serious attendant on public worship in the year 1798, but felt no peculiar impressions on her mind till the remarkable day in February, 1799.

The first thing that struck her mind powerfully, was a kind and serious message sent to her from her sister, who lived in a neighboring society. The message was this—"*Above all things get an interest in Christ.*" The effect was instant and surprising. She had heard the same thing before from her sister—nay, she had been exhorted repeatedly to the same purport, but to no effect. But now an impression was made, which nothing could efface. And there were many such instances on that day. Neither the common concerns of a family, the ridicule to which she would probably expose herself, the intervening of company, the suggestions of her former regularity of life, nor any considerations whatever, could withdraw her attention from the concerns of her soul and eternity. She had found she had been alive without the law; but the commandment came, sin revived, and she died. It appears from her own confession, made more than once, that though she frequently read the Bible, and would by no means, as she thought, omit any of the duties of religion, yet she never had any proper idea of the Bible, and knew nothing of the nature of the Christian religion; her understanding being so darkened as not to receive the things of the Spirit of God. But being now awakened, she continued in this state of anxious concern for thirteen or fourteen days, her distress increasing every day. Being a near neighbor, I had frequent opportunities of conversing with her, and of observing the operations of her mind; which I will relate, as I related them to the congregation in a sermon preached on account of her death.

She was one of the first that in this wonderful season of God's grace, was deeply impressed with the truth, respecting her depravity of heart, Christless state, and need of regeneration; and the first that was hopefully brought out of darkness into God's marvelous light. A day or two before this, her anxiety had increased to such a degree, that she could scarcely sleep at all, and her whole attention was absorbed in the thought of her sinfulness and perishing condition ; especially with the idea of the total opposition of her heart to God. She saw clearly that how much soever she attempted to pray, or to search the Scriptures, and whatever pains she took in a selfish way, she was guilty of breaking the first commandment, as she did not submit to the righteousness of God, and directly opposed the injunction of the apostle, " Whether ye eat or drink, or whatever ye do, do all to the glory of God." Hence she found that she was actually rising up against the will of Jehovah, and in no point, conformed to the spirit of the law signified in these words—" Thou shalt love the Lord thy God with all thy heart, and with all thy soul, and with all thy mind, and thou shalt love thy neighbor as thyself; " and therefore, she was under the just curses of that law. Exercises and views of this kind from day to day, filled her with great distress, and she began to despair of ever becoming religious according to the Bible requirements, and to conclude that there was no hope in her case—at best, that she never should, of herself, embrace the way of life ;— that she must, therefore, fearful as it was, fall into the hands of a sin-hating and sin-punishing God; that all her attempts were vain, all her endeavors fruitless, and that she was undone forever. At this time it pleased the Lord to afford her a view of the propriety of his dominion, and of the wisdom, rectitude and glory of his character and universal government. And the view was so clear that she was obliged to approve of the sentence of condemnation against herself, accept the punishment of her sins, and say, " Let this Lord be glorious. It is delightful that he is such a being, and that he reigns over me, and over all things. O how wicked have I been to oppose so glorious a God. I abhor myself, and may I and all creatures be heartily disposed to praise him forever."

These exercises were attended with immediate relief from her anxiety, and issued in the possession of a calm and peaceful state of mind, rejoicing, yet trembling, in the thought that God could and would do his own pleasure ; but would do nothing wrong, or contrary to the general good. This was her support. This calmness in the same views lasted three or four days, without much sensible joy in the expectation of eternal blessedness. The God of hope had not yet made her *to abound in hope through the power of the Holy Ghost;* nay, she seemed not to have the faintest idea that what she had experienced, was conversion. But on the fourth day, as she was listening to a sermon from these words, "Go into Galilee, there shall ye see him," in which the seeing of Jesus was described, the Lord was pleased to afford her such views and enjoyments, as she said exceeded all the joys that she ever had before. And Jesus, as the glory of God, and the Saviour of sinners, was the subject of her thoughts, her joys and her love, from that time till her dying hour, with very little interruption. Now she found one in whom she might fully confide to accomplish all things, not for her alone, but for the whole universe, in the best manner—one that united, harmonized, and illustrated all the perfections of the divine character in himself, while he was a suitable, a gracious and all-sufficient Saviour, just such an one as she needed.

These views and feelings were attended with an ardent and most affectionate consecration of herself, time, talents, and all things to the glory of the sacred Trinity, choosing to be his at all times, in all circumstances, and under every trial, and to be disposed of, as he might think proper.

These views gave energy to her desires that the glorious work among us might be carried on, and spread more and more. 'Twas her delight to hear of one and another brought under powerful convictions, and hopefully reconciled to God.

In her last sickness, the God of grace supported her amidst the excruciating pains which she endured without a murmur. I do not recollect that I ever saw greater resignation, calmness and rest in God, than appeared on her death-bed.

In one of my visits, she told me of the views she had just then had of the sufferings of Christ, and their effects upon her in producing calmness, self-loathing, cordial sorrow for sin, and adoration of his infinite condescension, such as the people of God frequently have at his table. These exercises, mixed with great love to the divine character, attended her, in a peculiar manner, through almost all her sickness. Once she found that her beloved Jesus had forsaken her. When she was supposed to be dying, and under this idea enjoyed the calmness of hope, and seemed to sink away, so that her father and all the attendants supposed her dead, it pleased the Lord to revive her, so that she lived a week longer. Upon reviving, she immediately thought that it was probable that she was reserved for further agonies, and felt a degree of unsubmissiveness. And the Lord withheld his shining countenance. She remained in darkness an hour or two—and then the Lord blest his Word for her relief, so that she exclaimed as well as her disorder would permit, "O those precious words, I cannot repeat them, but they are delightful. I am relieved." And this was her apparent frame of mind to the last.

A few minutes before she left the body, she uttered some of the most ardent petitions that this peculiar work which she had felt, might take hold of every heart in this place, spread more and more in the neighboring towns, through our land, and through the world. This work was peculiarly precious to her. She was afraid that many poor souls might be deluded with a morality like her own, and think that they had religion when they were in the gall of bitterness. On this account she could not praise the Lord enough for enlightening her eyes, nor could she cease to be jealous lest many like her, should be deceived with the form of religion without the power.

This, except what relates to her sickness and death, is the general complexion of the work among us. Three or four others were relieved the same week that she was, and although they had no opportunity of conversing together, or with any one that could inform them, yet they gave proof of the same work in each, attended only with a shade of difference as to manner and degree.

But lest it should be thought, that in this tender state of mind, they would be ready to receive any thing as truth which was said to them, and take any impressions that were wished, I must ask liberty to mention another instance. This was of a woman with whom I had no conversation from the time of her awakening, till she had experienced these very things. She was an active woman thirty-three years of age, always free to express her mind on religious topics, a resolute opposer of the doctrines of grace, and a person of good natural abilities. In her sentiments she was supported by her husband, who has now hopefully become a subject of this work, and who feels as though the doctrines which he opposed, are the only doctrines consistent with true peace of mind. I scarcely ever saw her, but she would introduce something in opposition to the distinguishing doctrines of the gospel. Our disputes were friendly, but I could never convince her of the truth.

She was somewhat unwell at the commencement of the revival; and as she lived about four miles from the place of public worship, she did not attend for several Sabbaths. One Sabbath in March as she was riding to meeting, she recollected that she had heard that there was a great *stir* among the people in other parts of the town, and she resolved to watch, and see if she could discover any thing uncommon. During the exercises of the forenoon, she discovered nothing new, except that the congregation was very still and solemn. There was no noise, nor confusion, which, according to her mistaken notions of an awakening, she expected to see. But at noon, she saw a number of young people coming to my house. She thought now she should discover all that she wished. She therefore followed them. When she came in, I was discoursing with the young people, and they gave manifest signs of alarm in view of their Christless, sinful and undone condition. At first she was struck with a sort of astonishment. But having reason to think that they really felt as they appeared to feel, she said to herself, "You poor sinner, see these young people, some of them not half so old as you. They have done nothing to what you have against God and his laws, and yet how distressed they are for their souls. And why am not I concerned? I have more reason than they. I know I am a sinner, and must perish if I remain so, but I have no feeling about it. Am I not left? O, these will go to heaven, and I shall go to hell. Lord, have mercy on me. What shall I do? I am undone forever." By this time she had forgotten to attend to what she could see in others. Her own concerns were enough. The great things of eternity engrossed her mind. The afternoon services were attended differently from any that she had ever attended before; and she was serious from this time till her dying hour, which was in October following. About three weeks after her first impressions, having heard of her distress, I visited the house. I found she had been relieved a day or two before. While she was talking and telling me how she was awakened, and what had been her feelings, I was almost amazed and transported. To hear her describe the whole from first to last,—what were her first impressions—her subsequent convictions—her endeavors to help herself, and patch up a righteousness of her own—how she was irresistibly convinced that she was perfectly helpless, sinful and wretched—to hear her so heartily approve of those doctrines which she had before so strenuously opposed, saying, they must be true—she knew some of them by experience, and others were absolutely necessary for the recovery of the soul;—and at the same time, knowing that she had no one particularly to instruct her on these points, were circumstances as wonderful as ever I had seen or heard. Such confirmation of what I believed to be the doctrines of the gospel, and poured into her mind with such marks of omnipotent mercy;—made me rejoice, and tremble too. Could I doubt of the work, or who was the author? I should as soon doubt who made the sun and planets.

This, and a number of other similar cases, induced me to cry out to myself, "Stand still and see the salvation of God."

The cases which have now been mentioned, are only specimens of the work in general, the greatest part being affected in the same way, and with the same truths, attended with a difference only as to time, means and degree.

But there are some others, which though they were grounded on the same truths, and issued in the same peace and joy, were nevertheless in some respects singular.

A man more than thirty years of age, who had been very intent upon gaining this world, was rather displeased with what took place among us, and showed himself an opposer. He thought there was no need of so much attention. One day as he was at work, it came distinctly into his mind, "You must pray." "I can't pray." "But you must pray." "I can't, for the prayer of the wicked is sin." "But you must pray." Thus a sort of dialogue continued for a long time between his conscience and his wicked heart. It was renewed again the next day, and the day following, and so on for nearly a week, when the impression became so great that he finally gave in that he must retire and make a business of prayer. The next day, or next but one after this point was settled, he was attacked in the same manner by his conscience as distinctly as if some one spoke to him. "You must pray in your family." "O no, that I can't do." "But you must do it." "No, it is not necessary; it is not command." "But it is your duty, and you must do it." Thus the dialogue continued for almost another week, and finally he was obliged to yield. But not being, in heart, disposed to comply, and not being accustomed to pray, he became very uneasy, and one kind of guilt and another, from time to time, starting up in his mind, he began to be greatly distressed; yet he determined no one should know it. He used all his art to suppress his feelings, especially before the people. But nothing would answer. He was obliged to own himself a hell-deserving creature, before the face of all; and after a season of powerful conviction and heavy distress, he found comfort in submitting to God.

Another man, thirty-five years of age, respectable for his good sense and judgment, is also an instance which I would mention. He was at first disaffected to the work that was among us. He had opposed the distinguishing doctrines of the gospel, not because he did not see them in the Bible, but through a disrelish of them. He contrived to think, that possibly there was some wrong translation, or that some words had been foisted in by designing men; and with this imposition on himself, rested easy concerning them. Being about to preach at his house, the latter part of March, I asked him if in this serious time, he felt any peculiar impressions on his own mind? He answered that he had not. I then asked him if he had not lately thought more on serious subjects? He said that he had, and that he did not believe there was a man in town who had not. But he appeared no more concerned for his soul, than the generality of people at other times. In reading over my text, the latter part of which was, " Who hold the truth in unrighteousness," almighty God impressed him with a conviction that he was the very man—that he had held the truth in unrighteousness. In the course of the sermon, he came to the fixed resolution to reform, and lead a better life. He felt it important to delay no longer, and that the salvation of his soul was of immediate and infinite importance. He attended meeting in the evening, when his resolution was strengthened. But as he was walking home alone, so earnestly engaged and resolute, the Spirit of the Lord gave him an extraordinary sense of his perfect weakness and insufficiency, and indeed of the total moral depravity of his heart; and the conviction was so clear, that all his hopes were dashed to pieces; and he became fully sensible, that nothing but the grace of an almighty Sovereign could help him. But whether such a vile, ungodly, obstinate sinner as he was, could ever partake of that grace, was matter of great doubt and anxiety. He almost despaired of it, and spent the whole night in horror, without a moment's sleep. The next day he attempted to labor, but his mind was too much absorbed in the view of his certain guilt and exposedness to everlasting ruin, to allow it. He attended a lecture, hoping to receive that help, and those good affections which he knew he ought to have. But in this he was disappointed. Instead of having his heart melted and mended, he found it more unfeeling and inattentive, for he looked to the means, and not to the God of salvation. This increased his sense of danger. He debated whether it would be best to attend the evening meeting, lest he should be made still more unfeeling; but finally concluded he would attend. Here, also, he found himself more stupid than before, and began to conclude that nothing could affect him—that God would most certainly refuse his grace; and he thought he justly might. Then a sense of the all-powerful and all-seeing God made him tremble in every part. He slept none this night. In the morning, after some ineffectual attempts to attend upon his secular concerns, he thought of visiting me. He came, but found no relief. In the afternoon, he heard a sermon at a funeral, but this seemed rather to harden him—a merciful God in all these attempts, showing him the desperate wickedness of his heart, the insufficiency of human aid, and cutting him off from every dependence, but his own infinite grace. He became more and more sensible of his wretchedness, and the sources of that wretchedness. He found that his deceitful heart would look to any thing but to God through Christ, for help. Hence he concluded that it was perfect enmity against God; and that if God did not appear in a way of sovereign mercy, he must perish eternally.

This evening, being exhausted, he had an hour or two of broken sleep, but awaked to keener feelings. He felt himself, all night, in a most forlorn situation. About the dawn of day, he had some new views of the propriety of submitting to God unconditionally; and that it was a thing most suitable and excellent that Jehovah should do his pleasure concerning all things. His obstinacy now gave way. He thought he could acquiesce in the divine Sovereignty, and immediately found relief. The thought that all God's administrations were perfectly holy, just and good—that he would do nothing but what the best interests of the universe required, gave him a calmness of mind to which he had been a perfect stranger. But all this time it did not enter into his mind that he should be saved. On the contrary, it was his prevailing opinion that he must be rejected; for the wrath of God was revealed from heaven against him. As soon as it was light enough to see, he read a few verses in the Bible, and set out to walk a small distance; but the powerful impressions on his mind, induced him to stop a moment. In this moment, a number of texts of Scripture came to him as distinctly, as if they had been spoken by some other man; such as these— "Come unto me, all ye that labor and are heavy laden"—"Ho every one that thirsteth," &c., and some others, which he did not recollect to have read or heard for a long time. He now concluded that it was the Lord of Glory addressing his Word to him. But the inference was not such as proud and self-conceited fanatics would draw—namely, that he should be saved, for God was now his friend. On the contrary, he concluded that Jesus addressed him in this manner, to show him the aggravation of his condemnation. And his reflections were most bitter. "O what a Saviour I have rejected—how able and ready has he been to save me—but I have rejected him, and held all his truths in unrighteousness. Eternal death is my portion, in spite of all the love and merits of Jesus. He has in perfect justice turned against me, and I cannot open my mouth to complain." With reflections like these, he walked backwards and forwards a few minutes, wringing his hands in fearful agony, as being now certain of his miserable doom for eternity. At this time, these words came into his mind as distinctly as the others— "Have I not done enough for you? Have you not stood against me long enough?" An overcoming power attended these words, so that he was constrained to cry, "Yes, O yes, Lord, I bow to thee; O make me what thou wilt."

This was succeeded by a serenity and peace which he never felt before, and of which he had no idea. It was divine refreshment to a soul dissolved in penitence and love.

The day before this, he told a friend that it seemed to him, that if he should ever be so happy as to obtain an interest in Christ, he could never pray in his family, because he was such an ignorant and helpless creature. But this morning he soon returned to his house, called his family together, and poured forth such strains of adoration and acknowledgment, and such fervent prayers, as melted the family into tears. I will only add, that his apparent perseverance gives reason to believe that his hope was not a mere delusion.

CHAPTER IX.

An account of a Revival of Religion in GOSHEN, CONN., in the year 1799. By the REV. ASAHEL HOOKER.

SUNDRY persons, whose knowledge of the subject is correct, have informed me, that previous to my settlement in this place, there never was any remarkable and extensive revival of religion among the people. There were, however, some signal instances of the power of divine grace.

Since my fixed residence here, which is almost nine years, things have remained in the most unpromising state, as to the interests of religion, with a little exception, till about the middle of February, 1799. That period, however, was rendered memorable by the commencement of a work, the happy fruits of which are still apparent, and which I trust will be lasting as eternity. From small beginnings, it made such progress in a few weeks, as to have arrested general attention; while great numbers were under the most serious and impressive sense of their forlorn state as sinners. Public worship on the Sabbath, and all other meetings appointed for religious purposes, were unusually attended, both as to numbers and seriousness. Many seemed anxious, and in great earnest to know what they should do to be saved. It was not long before sundry persons manifested a hope of having passed from death unto life. In the compass of a few months their number became considerable, and continued still increasing. In the month of September, *twenty-five* persons were admitted to the church; in November, *forty-eight;* and in January, *four;* making in the whole seventy-seven. A considerable number remain still, who exhibit the usual evidence of a new heart, who have not made a public profession of their faith. The visible change which has been wrought in many, is great and wonderful. Those who gave precious evidence of friendship to the Redeemer and his cause, seemed to say, with one voice and ineffable joy,—"This is the Lord's doing, and it is marvelous in our eyes."

After this brief statement, the following remarks will exhibit the distinguishing features of this work, and enable the candid and impartial to judge for themselves, whether it be indeed the Lord's work, and worthy of its reputed author.

1. It is worthy of notice, that numbers were deeply impressed before they were apprised that any others were in like circumstances. Impressions did not seem to be generally imparted from one to another. Frequently, without the intervention of any means which could be distinctly recollected, the truth and reality of eternal things, were brought home and fastened on their minds with a sort of irresistible and impressive weight, pointing them to the vast importance of fleeing from the wrath to come. This evidently was not the work of enthusiasm, nor but slightly, if at all, tinctured with it.

2. The first impressions on the minds of those who were the subjects of the work, did

not, in common, consist chiefly of fears, excited by the dreadful forebodings of future punishment. It was apparent that their most deep and painful impressions arose especially from convictions of sin, by which they were set at variance with themselves, and their past conduct as sinners; and by which it was awfully realized to them that "there is no peace to the wicked." It is worthy of particular mention, that those who became eventually reconciled to the truth, and found a comfortable hope of their good estate, were led to such an acquaintance with the plague of their own hearts, as served to subvert all hope, arising from themselves and their own doings. They were thence shown that if saved, it must be, not by works of righteousness which they had done, or could do, but "by the washing of regeneration, and the renewing of the Holy Ghost."

3. Where the foregoing convictions were brought to a happy issue, relief and comfort were found, in some sort, very differently from what was expected. The comfort and joy of the subjects seemed not to arise primarily from an apprehension that they were brought into a safe and happy state, but from new and delightful views of God, of the Redeemer, and the great truths which pertain to his kingdom. It

is hence remarkable, that frequently the subjects of the work seemed to be brought out of darkness into marvelous light, and to experience the sublime joys of religion, before they conceived any distinct hope of having become new creatures. It was hence rendered hopeful, that this *joy* was not *selfish* and *delusive*, as it could not have arisen primarily or chiefly from an apprehension of their own good estate. They, therefore, seemed frequently to lose sight of themselves, and their own particular interest, while contemplating the glory of God, as exhibited in the face of Jesus Christ.

It is worthy of particular notice, as a distinguishing feature of the late work in this place, that those who have been the hopeful subjects of it in its saving effects, notwithstanding their foregoing prejudices and opposition, have come uniformly and with one consent, into the scheme of doctrines understood by the general term *Calvinism*. These are the doctrines which seem to have been specially owned and blessed by the Holy Spirit, and thence made the wisdom of God and the power of God, to the salvation of sinners.

4. The subjects of this work were, in some respects, exceedingly various, as to their previous character and circumstances. A large

proportion of the whole number were those who had been educated in habits of general respect for religion, for the Sabbath, and public worship. Of these, some were evidently going about to establish their own righteousness, not regarding the necessity of a new heart, and of being clothed with the righteousness which is of God, by faith. In a few instances, those who had made a public profession of religion, were convinced that they were still in the gall of bitterness, and in the event, hopefully established in holiness. Others had been, for several years, if not always, in the habit of paying little respect to religion in any form. A considerable number, were more or less immoral and irreligious in their visible conduct. Several, who were scoffers at the serious and universal strictness of true religion, and who made light of the attention on its first appearance, were afterwards among the hopeful subjects of genuine conviction, and of saving mercy. A few, who had endeavored to fortify themselves against the fears of the wrath to come, in the belief of universal salvation, were convinced that they had made lies their refuge. Several, on whom the work was productive of the most evident, and apparently, most salutary and abiding effects, had been skeptical, and much inclined to infidelity.

If we take for granted, that the work which has been so far described, is a work of the Holy Spirit, one remark which naturally occurs, is the evident design of Providence to confound all attempts which should be made by philosophy and human reason, at accounting for the effects wrought, without ascribing them to God, as the marvelous work of his Spirit and grace.

5. It is not common for those who manifest a hope for themselves, to be very confident of their title to salvation. There are few, if any, but seem at times in much doubt whether their names are written in heaven. One reason of this, is plain. It is not usual for those who are hopeful subjects of mercy, to seem wise in their own conceits, or to have high thoughts of their own experiences, and attainments in religion; but in lowliness of mind, to esteem others better than themselves.

6. The subjects of this work are apparently disposed to persevere,—to run with patience the race set before them, and to give evidence of their union to Christ, by keeping his commandments.

How the things above stated will appear, when examined by the light and evidence of future days, and whether the hopes of Christians will be fully realized in the precious and abiding fruits of the wonderful things which they have seen and heard, must be left to future decision. Whether all those who appear to have set out, and to run well for the present, will hold on their way, and obtain the prize of their high calling, must be finally known by the event. The idea is cherished, with animated hope, that they will be to His praise in the earth, and the happy instruments of extending His kingdom among men. Of him, and through him, and to him, are all things, to whom be glory forever. Amen.

CHAPTER X.

An account of a Revival of Religion in Lenox, Mass., in the year 1799. By the Rev. Samuel Shepard.

I cannot learn from any of the first settlers that there has ever been any remarkable revival of religion in this town, until the month of June, 1799. It appears that the greatest number added to this church in the course of one year, was about eleven. This, if I am rightly informed, was the year 1783. At the time of my ordination, which was April, 1795, the situation of this church called for the earnest prayers of all who had a heart to pray. The number of its members then was not much greater than it had been for twenty-five years before; and almost the whole of them were bowing under the infirmities of age. No person, who was in early life, was a member of this church. Not a single young person had been received into it, in the course of sixteen years. To see the youth, all as one, wasting away their best moments in stupidity—to view them as accountable creatures, and yet living apparently without a hope—" without a wish beyond the grave"—and to see a few gray-headed persons compose almost the whole number of communicants at the sacramental table—must, to one just entering on the work of the ministry, awaken feelings which cannot be easily described. Well might this church, like God's ancient covenant people, when they sat in captivity by the waters of Babylon, hang its harps upon the willows; for it seemed, indeed, that when the few who were rapidly hastening down the vale of time, should be borne to the grave, and delivered from the evil to come, the name of Jesus, in the holy ordinance of the supper, would, among us, be scarcely had in remembrance.

Such were the melancholy prospects of this church until the spring of the year 1799. While showers of divine grace were falling on other parts of Zion, and God, by his Spirit, was visiting one place and another, and quickening multitudes for his name's sake, we seemed to be solemnly warned in the words recorded, Rev. 2: 5, " Remember, therefore, from whence thou art fallen, and repent, or else I will come unto thee quickly, and will remove thy candlestick out of his place." But the Lord hath said, " I will have mercy on whom I will have mercy ; " and glory be to his name. With him is the residue of the Spirit, and he can pour it out, when, and where, and on whom he pleaseth. He hath made it, therefore, a day of his power, and caused even in the midst of us, a shaking among the dry bones.

In the month of April, 1799, several members of the church manifested great anxiety about the state of religion among us, and expressed a desire that meetings might be appointed for religious conference and special prayer for the outpouring of the Holy Spirit. This request was afterwards made known to the church as a body. They unanimously approved of it, and a conference meeting was accordingly appointed. This meeting was attended by as many people, as previous appearances warranted us to expect. A sermon was preached at this meeting, and the audience were very attentive. At the next conference, we conversed upon a particular passage of Scripture, which led to a consideration of the being and perfections of God. Several persons at this meeting appeared unusually solemn. About this time, two or three young persons were brought under deep conviction, and found earnestly inquiring what they should do to be saved. At the third conference meeting, were to be seen persons from every part of the town. The divine authority of the Scriptures was made the subject of conversation, and the appearance of the assembly was truly affecting. They seemed now to consider the holy Bible to be the very voice of God to a guilty world; and the religion of Jesus, a solemn reality. Sinners were brought to tremble in view of eternity, and professors of religion were animated and rendered fervent in prayer. From that time, the work became more general—religious conferences were multiplied—the house of God was thronged upon the Sabbath—and multitudes seemed to spare no pains in obtaining religious instruction. Several persons, in attempting upon a particular Sabbath, to sing the judgment anthem, appeared to be greatly distressed. A sermon, the design of which was to enforce the leading ideas contained in the anthem, was afterwards delivered from Acts 1: 11—" This same Jesus which is taken up from you into heaven, shall so come in like manner as ye have seen him go into heaven." A divine blessing seemed, in some measure, to attend the discourse; and while those who entertained a hope of a personal interest in Christ, seemed to be wrapped up in the contemplation of that glory and majesty of Zion's King which will be displayed in that all-important day to which reference is had in the anthem, some of the opposite character were apparently filled with awful apprehensions on account of their ill-desert, and seemed to look forward to the day of judgment, as a time when their hearts must die within them. From that solemn season, there was an increasing attention to things of a serious nature, among young and old, for several months. While we heard of some from time to time, who were brought to a sense of their guilt and danger, others, having seen the impending storm of divine vengeance, and fled to one false refuge after another, till all were tried in vain, were hopefully brought to the foot of divine Sovereignty—to see the moral beauty, and transcendent amiableness and worth of the divine Saviour—to embrace him on gospel terms, and to find by experience that wisdom's ways are pleasantness.

On the twentieth of October, twenty-four persons were received into the church. This was with us a memorable day. But a small part of the congregation had ever before seen a young person publicly engage in the Christian warfare. From the same youthful circle—from the same family, some were taken, while others were left. While some parents were so happy as to see their children following them in the Christian profession, others, who were conscious of being still heirs of that kingdom which is doomed to destruction, saw their offspring fleeing for refuge to the wounds of a bleeding Saviour. Husbands and wives—parents and children—brothers and sisters, were separated by that line of distinction which is formed by a religious profession. In this, the divine Sovereignty was obvious. " The Lord reigneth, let the earth rejoice." Having taken upon themselves the bonds of the Christian covenant, and heard a particular address to the church and them dictated by the interesting occasion, those who in this public manner had united with the visible church of Christ, sang a hymn which concluded thus:

> "Saints by the power of God are kept,
>   Till full salvation come;
> We walk by faith, as strangers here,
>   Till Christ shall call us home."

The language to the spectators, in the scene then passing before them, was, "We are journeying to the place, of which the Lord said, I will give it you; come thou with us, and we will do thee good; for the Lord hath spoken good concerning Israel." A solemn silence was observed during the whole service. No appearance of levity was discovered, for a moment, in a single countenance. The infidel and abandoned man stood appalled—and, to the friends of Zion, the season afforded a prelibation of heavenly joys. The old and the young who were present, seemed ready to adopt the language of Jacob, when he awoke from a dream at Bethel, "How dreadful is this place! This is none other but the house of God, and this is the gate of heaven."

It was not till several months after this precious season that the attention began to abate. The whole number of those who have been received into the church since the work began, is fifty-three. Almost two-thirds are females. Many are in early life. Nearly all of them continue to give satisfactory evidence that Christ is, in reality, formed in them, the hope of glory.

In a time of ingathering like this, however, it is to be expected that some chaff will remain with the wheat. "Let not him that girdeth on his harness, boast himself as he that putteth it off." It becomes all those who engage in the Christian warfare, to remember that the promise of salvation is to him that endureth to the end; and that the same grace which at first called them, is requisite to their perseverance. "The fruit of the Spirit," says the apostle, "is in all goodness, and righteousness, and truth;" and "every man who hath" the Christian "hope in him purifieth himself even as he" who is the author of it "is pure."

The conduct of those who attended religious conferences and lectures, and for a time appeared to be seriously impressed, but afterwards returned to their former stupidity, forcibly reminds me of the case of one mentioned in Matt. 12: 45—"The last state of that man," said the Saviour, "is worse than the first."

The condition of those who remained uniformly careless and inattentive, while the goings of God were so visible among us, appears to be still more dangerous and deplorable.

I will close this general account with a few particular remarks.

1. This revival was evidently the work of

God. To prove this, the very sudden change in the appearance and pursuits of the people, is instead of a thousand arguments.

2. This revival began in the church; and I believe it will be found to be true, that in almost every instance of religious attention, it makes its first appearance in the church of Christ. When God is about to bestow spiritual blessings upon a people, it is his usual method, first to awake his professed friends out of sleep.

3. Such a revival of religion most strikingly evinces the importance of all the means of grace, which God hath instituted. When once the attention of a people is called up to the concerns of the soul, how precious, in their view, are seasons for prayer. How precious is God's holy Sabbath—how instantly do they fly to the Bible—how highly do they prize every opportunity to get religious instruction, and to associate with the people of God for serious conversation. God works by means in the moral, as well as the natural world. They are necessarily connected with the end. Faith cometh by hearing, and hearing by the Word of God.

4. The appearance of the people in this place at the time of the late awakening, will enable me to add to the testimony of others respecting the work in general, that it has been attended with

remarkable regularity. God was emphatically in the still small voice. Nothing was said, in particular, about dreams and visions—hearing unusual voices, and seeing uncommon sights. No extravagance, either in gestures or outcries, appeared. No wild enthusiasm attended the revival in any stage of it.

5. Among those in this town who have been awakened to attend to religious truths, a remarkable uniformity has occurred relative to the doctrines which have been embraced. These are such as are usually termed *Calvinistic*. Such truths as the total and awful depravity of the human heart—the necessity of regeneration; or a change of heart as a preparation for the enjoyment of a holy heaven—the equity of the divine law in its *penalty*, as well as *precept*—the divine sovereignty in the salvation of sinners, as the only possible ground of hope in the case of a guilty offender—the necessity of gospel morality, as an evidence of justifying faith—and all the doctrines essentially connected with these, were readily received by all with one consent.

6. It is worthy of notice that the revival of religion in this town, has proved to be almost a *death-wound* to the vain amusements of the

school among us in the time of the late special attention, was rendered nearly abortive; and the youth in general are still remarkable for their sobriety.

7. One distinguishing feature of this work as it appeared among us, and elsewhere, according to the narrations which have been published, was humility. The subjects of the revival, who have obtained a Christian hope, have very uniformly appeared to be humble, and to walk softly before their Maker. In view of the divine perfections and requirements, they have, at times, expressed great self-abhorrence. This has been one striking effect of the genuine operation of the divine Spirit on the hearts of sinners in every age.

May a holy God, in infinite mercy, continue to make manifest the glory of his power, and the glory of his grace, in building up Zion; for in no other way can we rationally hope to see happy individuals—happy families—happy neighborhoods—happy societies—happy towns—happy states—happy kingdoms—and a happy world.

CHAPTER XI.

An account of a Revival of Religion in FARMINGTON, CONN., in the year 1799. By the Rev. JOSEPH WASHBURN.

IN the fall of the year 1793, and through the winter following, while the society was destitute of a settled minister, there appeared, as I have been informed, peculiar attention to the means of grace, and a hopeful prospect of a time of a great refreshing from the presence of the Lord. But the hopes of the people of God, were greatly damped, and the work apparently interrupted, by means of an unhappy contention which took place in the society, and which threw the minds of the people into a state of high irritation. But the good Spirit of God, though grieved, did not wholly depart; and about the time of my ordination, which was in May, 1795, an uncommon attention and seriousness became apparent throughout the society. The divine influences came down like the dew, and like the rain upon the mown grass, in still and gentle showers. The work was unattended with noise or enthusiasm—caused a general solemnity through the society, and met with little or no opposition.

Within the course of about one year, fifty-five persons were added to the church.

In the fall of 1798, religion was apparently but little thought of except by some of the professed people of God, and even among them, an unusual degree of lukewarmness seemed to prevail. The distressing reflection now arose, that as we had been favored with a gracious visit of God, and had so soon grieved away his Spirit, it was to be feared that religion would now continue to decline for many years—and that if it should thus decline for ten or twenty years, as it had done for two or three, the situation of Zion, here, must be deplorable indeed.

At this time, God began to appear in power and great glory, in a number of towns in the vicinity, as he had done for a year before, in places more distant. An account of these things reached us, and became the subject of conversation among Christians; but it appeared to have little or no effect.

The first appearance of special divine power and grace, was in Feb., 1799. It began in an uncommon attention and concern among the people of God, in view of the situation of this society, and a disposition to unite in prayer for the divine presence, and a revival of religion.

Soon after this, numbers, in different parts of

the society, began to inquire respecting the meetings, and expressed a wish to attend. This was considered an omen for good, and upon the encouragement which now began to appear, it was determined to open lectures at the meeting-house, and at some of the school-houses, in the extreme part of the society. From this time, we had frequent meetings which were attended by great numbers. Persons of both sexes, and of almost every age, and many from the distance of four or five miles, and some still further, were to be seen pressing through storms, and every obstacle, to attend the meetings—such was their anxiety to hear the Word of God, and to know what they must do to be saved.

My house was also the almost daily resort of youth, and others earnestly inquiring respecting the things of their peace. The scenes were frequently very affecting. Persons from 12 or 15 up to 30 or 40 years of age, had just discovered, as to any realizing sense, that they were sinners. They felt, and in tears acknowledged, that they were under the condemnation of God's righteous law—that they had, all their lives, neglected and despised a kind Saviour, and trodden under foot, his blood. Those of the youth who were seriously impressed, now reflected on their former gayety, vanity and sinful amusements, with bitterness and entire disapprobation. They considered the customs and practices commonly followed by youth as very dangerous and pernicious—tending to exclude the thoughts of God and eternity—cherish vicious propensities—render the mind light and vain—and inconsistent with doing all things to the glory of God. An attempt which was made soon after the awakening commenced, to introduce a dancing master, and set up a school for the instruction of the youth and children in the art of dancing; and which, though, with much difficulty, at length, succeeded, had a happy effect on the minds of some of the serious youth, tending to increase their impressions. The open opposition, also, which was made by some, had a similar effect. It convinced them more and more, that madness is in the heart of man, and that God is just in condemning sinners and casting them off forever.

About one hundred have been so far impressed as to inquire seriously and anxiously respecting the way of life by a Saviour, and to converse freely upon the state of their souls. Of these, about seventy have appeared to be under deep conviction of sin, and in great distress of mind.

Sixty-one have been admitted to the church within one year, viz: from August, 1799, to

August, 1800. Several who have not made a profession of religion, have it in contemplation, and it is to be hoped that there are some others, who have become truly reconciled to God.

After this general account of the progress and extent of the work, a more particular statement of the personal views and exercises of those who have been the subjects, either of conviction or hopeful conversion, will be necessary.

In the first stages of concern, the subjects were generally most affected with particular sins, and not so deeply sensible of the plague of their own hearts. As the work of conviction proceeded, they obtained a clearer view of the spiritual nature and extent of the divine law, and a more realizing sense of the corruption of their hearts. It was generally the case with those under deep conviction, that they in a greater or less degree, experienced sensible enmity, and opposition of heart against the character of God—particularly his sovereignty in having mercy on whom he will have mercy, and hardening whom he will. There were several instances in particular in which a wise and sovereign God permitted the enmity and obstinacy of the carnal heart, to be manifested in an awful manner, and to an astonishing degree. While conscience like a gnawing worm preyed upon them within, a view of the divine character, and the way of salvation proposed in the gospel, excited the enmity of their hearts, and filled them with anguish; and every instance in which they saw any of their friends or acquaintance brought apparently to embrace the gospel, filled them with a kind of envy—with a pain which they could not describe.

With respect to the manner and circumstances in which the hopeful converts obtained relief, and the degree of their joy and peace, there has been a variety. Some few were very suddenly relieved from their distress, and filled with adoring, and admiring views of God and the divine Saviour. But with respect to the greater part, they were brought very gradually to entertain a hope that they were reconciled to God, and did not soon attain to any considerable degree of rejoicing, or assurance of hope. The hopeful converts, in general, have appeared very far from a disposition to think highly of themselves, or their attainments in religion, and especially from a spirit of rash judging, or censuring others. They appear to be disposed to hope the best of others—to promote the good of all—to discharge relative and social duties—to attend carefully upon all the institutions of religion, and to manifest a tender regard for the salvation of souls, and the advancement of the cause of God in the world.

I shall now give a summary account of several particular cases.

The first is of a man about 30 years old; of a religious family, and of a good understanding. He was in the view of the world, a good man— a praying man; and one who was not considered by any who were acquainted with him as inclined to be enthusiastic, or subject to any uncommon dejection, or gloominess of mind. As he had enjoyed special advantages by means of a religious education, to know himself, and be influenced to his duty, so he was called upon, and peculiarly tried by distressing and alarming providences—particularly by the very sudden death of his two only sons, within a few days of each other, in the fall of 1798. This distressing scene awakened him to some concern, and attention at first, but it very soon passed off, and he became as careless and inattentive as ever— living, however, as before, in the formal observance of family religion, and external morality. At length, in the month of February following, God was pleased by his almighty Spirit, to fix that conviction of sin, and sense of guilt on his mind which the most powerful means, and awakening calls of God's providence and Word, had not been able to do. From this time, I shall give the exercises of his mind as I took them from his mouth.

"I was first awakened at a lecture in a neighboring society. I was in great distress under a sense of sin, and my distress continued and increased for two or three weeks, when I found a sermon by Dr. Doddridge upon the diversity of the operations of the Spirit. Before this I had no idea that I had experienced any thing of true religion; but after reading that book, I began to feel more easy. For several days, I thought I loved to pray and to read the Scriptures. But the next Sabbath I heard a discourse which in some measure, confounded me. The design of it was, to describe the nature of true religion, and distinguish it from that which originates in selfishness. The observations appeared to be just and Scriptural, and yet to be against me. A few days after this, I began to have heart-risings against God, and was filled with pain and opposition, whenever I saw others appear to delight in God and religion. After this, I had a greater sense of the plague of my heart, than ever before. My mind had been more fixed before this, upon particular outbreakings of sin. But now I was led to a sight and sense of the fountain of wickedness within me, from which all had flowed—and I was convinced that I was an enemy to God. Before this, when I thought or spoke of my sins, I often shed tears; but now I was unable to weep. I considered this at that time, as the effect of a greater degree of hardness and stupidity. And it appeared to me to be occasioned by conversing with Christians and ministers. The more I conversed with them, the more hard and unfeeling I seemed to grow; and it was suggested to my mind that I had better wholly avoid them.

About the first of April, my distress of mind was so great, that I had no appetite for food, and could get but little rest by night or day. For about two months I rarely slept more than half an hour or an hour in the night. In several instances, I spent the whole night without sleep, in great agony of mind, looking one way and another for relief. At one of these times, my mind turned upon the subject of the truth of the Scriptures. I queried whether there was not some ground to hope that the Bible would prove to be false. It appeared that if I could believe there was, it would give me relief; but I could not for a moment. I knew and felt it to be the truth and the word of God, though I had no love for it. I could therefore find no relief; but was filled with such an apprehension of the miseries of the damned, that I thought I should lose my reason. My health was now brought so low, by means of the anguish of my mind, and want of rest, that I was obliged entirely to desist from labor, and apply to a physician. And as I viewed myself one of the greatest sinners in the world, I thought it likely God was about to take me out of the world, and destroy me as an example and warning to others. Indeed my distress was so great that I did not wish to live, and I began to be under temptations to destroy myself.

"Being at this time unable to attend public worship, I did not regret it; for preaching, or religious conversation, or whatever brought up the character of God, was exceedingly painful to me. I was unwilling also that my wife or friends should attend meeting, and I tried to prevent them; for I could not endure to have them or any others enjoy any comfort and satisfaction in religion. The happiness of others in religion, and the service of God, was a source of torment to me. I found also, as I thought, that I did not love my friends; and that I had not that regard and tenderness for my wife and child which I used to have. And whenever I heard of any person being of a good disposition, it would cause my heart to boil with a kind of envy.

"After I had arrived at this pitch, I would willingly have given ten thousand worlds, if it had been in my power, to have been deprived of my reason. My conscience stung me so that I should have been willing to change circumstances with a toad, or the meanest and vilest creature that ever was. I would have given any thing to be put out of existence. I thought if I knew that thousands of years would end the miseries of hell, it would give me some relief. I thought if I could justify myself, and cast the blame upon God, this would relieve my distress. But I felt this to be impossible; and I saw my heart so opposed to God, that I concluded I was left by his Spirit, and was in an unpardonable state. A great part of the time, I was in total despair, and thought I felt as miserable as the damned. No one who has not experienced it, can have any idea of the distress which I endured. I don't think but that I could have sat down and put both my feet into the fire, and held them there, and bore the pain more easily than to bear what I did in my mind.

"I continued in this state of mind from the forepart of August till the latter part of September, or beginning of October. About this time, I began to entertain some hope that I was reconciled to God. I thought I could take pleasure in meditating on the divine character, and those doctrines of the gospel, which had once been so painful. It appeared that all God's ways were right, and all his requirements reasonable, and that it would be the greatest happiness to be able to serve him. Soon after, I heard a sermon from the words, 'My grace is sufficient for thee.' It was a text and subject which came with great power and comfort to my mind; and it appeared now more than ever to be reasonable and desirable to submit myself into the hand of God, to be disposed of by him as he pleases."

Upon being asked whether he could fix upon any particular time in which he was renewed and humbled, if ever—he replied, "I cannot; and I often have great fears that I never have been truly humbled. But, at times, if my heart does not deceive me, I feel a happiness in meditating on the character of God, and in the thought that I am in his hands, and that all things are at his wise disposal. And though for the most part, I indulge a hope in his mercy through Jesus Christ, yet I am sensible that in myself I am infinitely unworthy, and ill-deserving; and that it would be perfectly just and righteous in God to cast me off. And if this should be my portion, and it should finally appear that I had been left for my great wickedness, to deceive myself with a false hope, I could have nothing to say."

Upon being asked what his present feelings were, towards careless, impenitent sinners, he replied, "I feel that they are to be pitied. It seems when I reflect upon it, as if I could not bear the thought of any one going on, and finally suffering such a hell as I have tasted. An eternity of such distress as I experienced for a time in my breast, by a view of the divine character, and the happiness of others in serving God, would be intolerably dreadful."

Another person, rising of 20 years of age, gave me a narrative, of which the following is an abstract.

"My advantages have been great from a child; and I have often had some concern of mind respecting religion; but nothing very special, till the time of the religious attention in this society four or five years ago. I was then considerably impressed, but my concern soon left me in a great measure, and I lived in a state of carelessness and stupidity, till the beginning of the fall of 1798. About this time, a solemn providence was made the means of alarming me, and awakening my attention to my spiritual condition and prospects. My anxiety for a time was great; but it was not long before I began to entertain a hope that I was in a safe state, and was much relieved. But soon I became convinced that I was in the gall of bitterness and bond of iniquity; and that my hope had been without any just foundation. My anxiety, therefore, returned, and continued more or less till the winter following. In February, before any appearance of uncommon attention in the society, my conviction and distress of mind greatly increased. I had a clear sense of my sin, and experienced sensible opposition of heart to God, and to the doctrines of the gospel which I heard preached. I was convinced of their truth, and yet hated them. Often when I have heard them held up with plainness, in the house of God, on the Sabbath, I have wished that I could be absent. To be obliged to sit and hear things so disgusting, and which I knew to be the truth, was exceedingly painful. The Bible also, was to me a most odious book. I could not endure to read it. Every page appeared to be against me. While in this situation, I looked on every side for relief. I fled to every thing for refuge, but to God. For a time I strove hard to disbelieve the doctrines of the gospel. I searched diligently to find arguments against them—particularly the doctrine of the endless future punishment of the wicked. I listened to the arguments of the Universalists—I endeavored to persuade myself that God was such a merciful being that he never would punish any of mankind, or at least, not with endless punishment—whatever might be their treatment of him, and of his Son in this life. But all was in vain—the Scriptures were decisive—and I was obliged to acknowledge the necessity of religion, and of an interest in Christ, in order to any true peace in this, or another world. Accordingly I set myself very earnestly as I thought, to obtain it—labored hard to make my heart better, and to recommend myself to the Saviour. But finding all attempts of this kind fail, and finding that the opposition of my heart increased, I fled for refuge to antinomianism. I thought it must be impossible for a sinner to love God, as long as he supposed his sins were unforgiven, and that God was his enemy. I, therefore, endeavored to think that Christ had died for me, in particular, and that my sins were all pardoned;—hoping that if I could persuade myself of this, it would give me peace, and be unto me according to my faith, or as I now view it, my vain self-flattering. But I was not permitted to wrap myself up in this delusion. I next attempted to persuade myself that there was no such thing as free moral agency, or accountability, nor any distinction between virtue and vice—but that mankind were mere machines, actuated by a blind and fatal necessity. But I was unable to reason myself into a belief of this. I had a consciousness of sin and guilt which I could not throw off. I felt my desert of misery, and of the perfect reasonableness of my being required to give my heart to God. My heart, however, was still opposed,—his character and conduct I did not love—especially his leaving me in this situation when he was able to deliver me, and did deliver others, and give them hope and comfort. And whenever I heard of any particular instance of this, it caused the opposition of my heart to rise very high. I was told that I must submit. I attempted to do it, and to flatter myself that I did submit—But my submission would last no longer than till the character of God came clearly into view again. After these things, I had a lively sense of the hypocrisy I had been guilty of in every thing I had been doing—that in all my strivings, I had had no sincerity or regard to God; but had been actuated in every thing by perfect selfishness—that all my cries to God, had been mere mockery—flowing from a heart totally opposed to him—that in every prayer I had made for the Holy Spirit, God had seen that it was not from the heart; but that my heart and words were at perfect variance. Never before, had I such an idea of the plague of my heart, or of the sensible enmity against God, which an awakened sinner may be the subject of. My distress was now such that I thought I could not endure it. I slept but little; and whenever I awoke from sleep, my distress and anguish came upon me in a moment. I used to think that if I could be relieved for a few moments, it would be more tolerable. But I had no relief—and what added exceedingly to my distress, was the thought that it would probably not only be constant, but forever.

" But notwithstanding all my distress, I greatly dreaded the thought of falling back into my former stupidity—being convinced that if I was given up to carelessness, I should perish, and that the light and conviction I had resisted would greatly aggravate my condemnation.

" After continuing a while in this state, doubts began to rise in my mind, respecting the divinity of the Scriptures. I questioned whether the Bible was the word of God, and I even sometimes harbored the thought that there was no God. This, when I came to reflect upon it, increased, if possible, my distress. I viewed it as an evidence that I was left of God—and that I was about to be given up to delusion to believe a lie. I now began to despair of ever being brought to repentance. And for a considerable time, except at intervals, I chose death rather than to continue in life. I thought there was no happiness for me in this world, nor in the next—and that the longer I lived, the more intolerable would be my future misery. In these dreadful moments of despair, the most shocking temptations would rush upon me, urging me to destroy myself. But through the mercy of God, I was preserved from a compliance with them.

" While under these temptations, and during all the time of my greatest distress, I was very careful to conceal my feelings and exercises. For this purpose, I kept much alone, and endeavored to avoid conversation as much as possible. I felt ashamed, and afraid to let the state of my mind be known—judging from my own former views and feelings respecting such things, that were I to relate what I had experienced, no person would credit me; and that I should be considered either as delirious, or disposed to deceive. I am now fully convinced that my conduct, in this respect, was unwise and injurious. Had I freely opened my mind to some person acquainted with the exercises of sinners under conviction, and the devices of Satan to destroy them, I might have been much relieved under the despair and temptations I experienced, and perhaps wholly prevented from falling into them. But God is wise in all he has permitted to take place. And he is infinitely merciful; or when I was thus guilty of the heinous sin of despairing of his mercy, I should have been immediately destroyed.

"It was several months after I began to be delivered from that despair and peculiar distress which I have mentioned, before I entertained a hope that the enmity of my heart was subdued. I fix not on any particular time when this took place, if ever. I am far from being confident respecting myself. I know the heart is deceitful above all things, and desperately wicked. Yet, for the most part, I entertain a hope, grounded upon the submission and peace which, if I am not deceived, I sometimes find in contemplating the character of God, and the Saviour, and the truths and precious promises of his Word, and in a desire to be conformed to his holy will."

CHAPTER XII.

An account of a Revival of Religion in NORFOLK, CONN., in the year 1799. By the Rev. AMMI R. ROBBINS.

It pleased the blessed God, in the year 1767, to afford some special tokens of his gracious presence among us, to the peculiar joy of the precious few who loved Zion, and who wailed in fervent prayer for her prosperity. The blessed influences of the Spirit seemed to be shed down in a remarkable manner, and the whole town seemed to be awed with the presence of the Lord. Many were struck with surprise, and numbers were impressed with a sense of their guilty and ruined state as sinners, and began to cry, what must we do to be saved ? But alas, it was of short continuance, as to its power and abiding influence. A number, however, were so deeply impressed that they could find no relief, until they were hopefully made new creatures and found rest in Christ Jesus—about ten or twelve, who seemed to live like Christians, and joined themselves to the Lord ; while many who were awakened and terrified for a short season, fell back into stupidity, and some became in their lives and conduct worse than before. It pleased the God of all grace, to call in one and another successively for several years following, until the year 1783, which will be memorable with us, and, I trust, will be remembered by many with thanksgiving and praise through eternal ages. This second revival, if it may be so called, began in May, 1783, when it appeared, by inquiry afterwards, that some of God's people had been remarkably stirred up to pray for the outpouring of the Holy Spirit. Numbers were impressed in different parts of the town, without any knowledge of each other's circumstances, at the same time. The seriousness became general, and the distress of many visible. A public lecture was set up, and was attended nearly every week through the summer, at which some one or other neighboring minister attended, preached, and assisted in conversing with awakened and distressed souls after the meeting. Besides the public lecture, conferences were attended in different parts of the town. And such were the order and decency, in general, that those who sought occasion, if any there were, did not openly oppose the work. In consequence of this glorious day of divine grace, there were added to the church in November, twenty-seven; in the January following, thirteen; and in March, ten; making in all, fifty. Of these, eighteen were males, and thirty-two females. Besides these, several were added afterwards.

Most of these are still living, and with us, and we trust have walked agreeably to their Christian profession. By this means our church has been considerably numerous, and generally harmonious.

But it is to be lamented, that stupidity gradually increased and spread over the town. The wise and the foolish slumbered together.

Besides these gloomy appearances, some of the friends of Christ used frequently to remark, with distress and concern, that many of our younger people, and persons of information and influence, were fast verging towards infidelity. Several had nearly or quite renounced their belief in the divinity of the holy Scriptures, and others were reasoning themselves into the doctrine of universal salvation. Meanwhile profaneness increased like a flood, and various species of wickedness prevailed. So that it might be truly said of us that "iniquity abounded and the love of many had waxed cold." Amidst all this, it must be remarked that the people more generally came to meeting on the

Sabbath, and strangers would notice with surprise, that the general attendance of people on public worship was rather uncommon and extraordinary. But it is to be feared that the words of the prophet may with propriety be adopted concerning the most of them—"This people draw nigh to me with their mouth, and honor me with their lips, but their heart is far from me."

About five years ago, the concert of prayer proposed to be observed quarterly, and which was attended in many parts of the land, was also set up here, and the members of the church, with some others, attended. These seasons appeared to be solemn, and were animating and encouraging to numbers of God's people. But nothing special appeared, indicating a revival of religion, until January, 1799, when it was noticed that our religious assemblies were more solemn and attentive. The religious people about this time, hearing of some revivals of religion in two or three other towns in the vicinity, and having before this heard of the work of God at a further distance, were induced to hope, and ardently to pray that we might have a gracious visit also.

Although no special instances of awakening, as yet, appeared to take place, there is reason to conclude that numbers of God's dear people, in secret as well as in a social way, did most earnestly plead at the throne of grace, that the Lord would get glory to his name in reviving his work among us, and in infinite mercy send his Holy Spirit to arrest the progress of thoughtless sinners, who were in the broad way to eternal ruin. Soon it was whispered among some of our serious people, that one and another in this and that part of the town were troubled in mind. Our congregation on the Sabbath became more full than ordinary, and very solemn indeed. In February and March, the attention became so general that it was thought proper, at the desire of many, that religious conferences should be set up. They accordingly were, in four, and sometimes five different parts of the town. A public lecture was also appointed to be preached every Thursday, and became a matter of course through the summer, and into the autumn; so that there was no need of warning; but when the day came, the house was filled with people, almost like the Sabbath. Ministers from abroad were generally procured to preach on these occasions; and they were undoubtedly, by the blessing of God, a means of promoting the work, of instructing and edifying young converts, and guarding them against errors and intemperate zeal.

To give an account of the peculiar trials and exercises of individuals, would swell this narrative too much, and probably not be edifying to the bulk of your readers.

It may, however, be useful to observe, that as the Lord was about to carry on a glorious work of grace among us, it appears that he was pleased to begin it in a way that was suited to strike the people with surprise, and effectually stop the mouths of those who otherwise might oppose, or at least doubt of its being the Lord's work. For nearly at its beginning, there were several persons who were struck with a sense of their miserable state and condition as sinners. And although they tried hard, yet it was impossible for them long to conceal their feelings. Their very countenances would indicate clearly the distress of their souls. These were persons who were influential and very popular in town, and of very considerable information. They were, before this, very far from all appearance of religion—much inclined to, and some far advanced in deistical sentiments, and those of the universalists. These being hopefully subdued by an omnipotent arm, and appearing meek and humble in their deportment, gave a prodigious shock to many others, especially their intimates. And they now soon joined heart and hand to promote the work, by conversing with others, attending and assisting at conferences, and being enabled to conduct with modesty, humility and prudence, yet with firmness in the cause, were, no doubt, used as a happy means of promoting and spreading the religious attention.

In June and July, the marvelous displays of divine power and grace were conspicuous beyond any thing of the kind we had ever witnessed. A universal solemnity spread over the town, and seized the minds of almost all, both old and young. It appeared that Jehovah was, in very deed, in the midst of us, with a witness—yea, with many witnesses, sufficient to make even an atheist tremble. Great numbers were bowed with a sense of the presence of the Lord. Some rejoicing and praising God—others in anguish of soul, crying, what must we do? Yet they were by no means noisy or boisterous, but, in silent anguish, seemed to be cut to the heart.

Almost every day, we could hear of one or more who had found relief, or as the phrase was, "obtained a hope;" and new instances of persons impressed with a sense of their guilty, wretched, undone state.

Some appeared almost on the borders of despair, while others were complaining of a hard and obstinate heart, and that there could not be any sinner on this side hell so vile as they.

As there were now numbers who had for several months entertained hopes that they were reconciled to God, and friends to the Lord Jesus Christ, and being desirous to appear openly, if it might be, to espouse the cause, by making a public profession of religion, and observing all the ordinances of the gospel, it was thought best to give them opportunity. And this not only on their account, but as a means of the awakening and conviction of others. And here it must be observed, that numbers who had as yet remained unmoved, when they came to witness the solemn scene—when they beheld many of their intimate companions—a husband—a wife—a brother—a sister—a parent—a child—a near friend—a late jovial companion, with sweet serenity, solemnly giving up themselves to the Lord—publicly enlisting under the banner of Jesus, and engaging forever to renounce the ways of sin, and the corrupt practices of the world, and cleave to the Lord—and beholding one and another, at the same time, baptized in his name—they were pierced through, as it were, with a dart. They often went home full of distress, and could never find rest or ease, until they had submitted to a sovereign God, and placed their hope and confidence on Jesus Christ.

After due examination, they were admitted to full communion with the visible church. Aug. 11th, *sixteen* were admitted; Aug. 25, *twenty-four;* Oct. 6, *twenty-three;* Oct. 27, *twenty-two;* Dec. 15, *ten;* Jan. 19, 1800, *fourteen;* Feb. 2, *three;* March 16, *eight;* June 29, *three*, and Aug. 31, *eighteen*. Of these fifty-nine were males, and ninety-four females. Several others who entertain hopes respecting themselves, may probably soon be added.

Having given a brief sketch of the wonderful work of God among us, my feelings dictate that some remarks concerning it may be useful to comfort God's people, and to animate them in praying and laboring for the promotion of Christ's kingdom.

1. It is of unspeakable importance that the means of grace be used with impenitent sinners. Jericho's walls must tumble down in consequence of the blowing of the ram's horns. **Naaman must wash seven times in the waters**

of Jordan, that he may be cured of his leprosy. We have found by experience that not only the preaching of the Word, but religious conferences and social prayer-meetings, at which Christless sinners were present, have been abundantly blessed for the continuance of serious impressions on their minds, and increasing conviction of their heart-wickedness, and total insufficiency to help themselves.

2. Those doctrines which the world call *hard sayings*, are the most powerful means in the hands of the blessed Spirit to pull down and destroy Satan's strong-holds in the hearts of sinners. No preaching and conversation seems so effectual to drive them from their hiding-places and refuges of lies, as to tell them plainly that they are eternally undone, if the unpromised mercy of God is not displayed in their favor—that they have not the least claim on God, and if he does not have mercy, they are gone forever—that all which they do short of real submission to God, is wholly selfish—that they may as well despair of ever helping themselves first as last, and that the reason why they do not find relief is merely because they will not yield and bow to a holy sovereign God. I am sensible that some will be greatly irritated at these naked truths, and will not hear them.

But those whose eyes are open to see and realize eternal things, will be silent; and although they do not love these doctrines, they fear they are true, and appear to be cut to the heart.

3. When the subjects of this work were hopefully renewed, they were not usually sensible of it at the time—many of them not till some days afterwards. They perceived indeed an alteration in their feelings and views, but they did not entertain a thought that it was *conversion.* More generally they feared that God had left them, and that they had lost their conviction. Yet they have found upon reflection that God was right, and that they were wrong. They have agreed in this, that it would be just in God to cast them off, whatever he should do with others. A very sensible man, of middle age, told me with the greatest apparent sincerity, that it appeared to him, that for such a wretch as he, who had rebelled against, and insulted so great, so holy a God all his days, *hell* was the proper place—and that he did not see how God could do any other than send him there, and that he felt, that if he might love and praise him, he should be willing to be separated from that holy world where such wretches as he ought not to come. It has

been common for them to feel entirely submissive to God, and pleased with his administrations, while they did not imagine that they were interested in the atonement of Christ, or view themselves forgiven and accepted of God.

4. Before I close, it may be proper to make some observations respecting the fruits of this glorious work of God among us, as it is now almost two years since it began. The hopeful converts have generally appeared as well as could be expected. A spirit of love and union seems to prevail, as yet, among them. It is hoped that their religion will not be as the morning cloud and early dew which soon passeth away.

But after all, it is by no means designed by these communications, to represent, or to have it understood, that in such a glorious harvest there is not chaff among the wheat. It is greatly to be feared and expected that all will not persevere—that some will be found with the lamp of profession, but no oil in their lamp.

I will only add that there are a few instances of awakening now with us; and a number who are bowed down, and appear to be "weary and heavy laden."

One man nearly fifty years of age, who has been a member of the church for many years, more than a year ago gave up his hope entirely, viewed himself in an undone state—concluded there was no mercy for him, dared not come to the Lord's table, and was often filled with such agony, that he could hardly attend to the ordinary concerns of his family. Now it is hoped that his captivity is turned. He thinks he has entirely different views of God and the Redeemer from what he ever had before, and at times is filled with joy.

I hope and trust that thousands and thousands in heaven and earth, are, and will be employed in thanksgivings and praises to the triune God, Father, Son, and Holy Ghost, for the marvelous displays of his infinitely free, rich and sovereign grace among us here, as well as in many parts of our sinful land and world. And oh, let all that love our Lord Jesus and his cause, join as he has taught us, and with unceasing importunity devoutly and humbly pray, "Thy kingdom come, thy will be done on earth as it is in heaven."

CHAPTER XIII.

An account of a Revival of Religion in BRISTOL, CONN., in the year 1799. By the Rev. GILES H. COWLES.

FOR most of the time since my settlement in this place, there had been some individuals under serious impressions; and from six to eleven had been annually added to the church. But for a year or two before the revival began, the people appeared to be uncommonly inattentive to their eternal concerns. For more than a year, but one had made a public profession of religion, and not more than one appeared to be inquiring the way to Zion. The concerns of the present life, appeared to engross the attention of most. . . . . . . This was the situation of the society when the revival began in several neighboring places in the latter part of the year 1798. The minister of one of those societies preached here, the last Sabbath in January, 1799, and gave some account of the work of God in those towns, which considerably engaged the attention of the hearers, and appeared to affect the minds of some individuals. . . . . On the second Sabbath in

February, information was given that a lecture would be preached at the meeting-house on Wednesday, and that several ministers were expected. The people generally assembled, and three neighboring ministers were present. The exercises were introduced with some observations on the peculiar attention to religion which had begun in places around, and two sermons were delivered on the occasion. An unusual attention and solemnity were soon very apparent in the congregation, and numbers appeared deeply affected, and in tears. A conference being appointed in the evening, a large school-house was filled; and divine influences appeared more powerful than in the afternoon. The assembly was solemn as the grave. All seemed to be deeply impressed with a sense of the importance of their eternal concerns, and to hear with the most eager and anxious attention. The exercises continued till nine o'clock, and yet the hearers appeared as if unwilling to leave the house.

The next day, being on a visit in one part of the society, I conversed with three young persons who appeared to be feelingly convinced of their sin and danger, and who were the first that had any conversation with me respecting their eternal concerns. But within a week from the time of this lecture, perhaps fifty appeared to be under deep conviction of sin; and ten or twelve entertained a hope that they were reconciled to God. Thus the divine Spirit in its quickening influences, seemed to descend like a shower, in different parts of the society. Almost all appeared to be so far affected, that the general inquiry and conversation were about the things of religion. At first, it was in some, perhaps an affection of the passions, but as this subsided, it was in many instances succeeded by a deep and rational conviction of their guilt, danger, and need of the Saviour, and the renewing influences of his Spirit. For several months, the work of conviction continued to extend, though with less rapidity than at first, and there were frequent instances of hopeful conversions; till by some disagreeable occurrences, the work appeared to be greatly retarded in the month of June. At that time a sectarian controversy about certain sentiments, little connected with the essential truths of religion, unhappily arose, and for a time, engaged much of the attention and conversation. This produced disputes and ill-feelings, and seemed greatly to divert attention from that anxious concern for the salvation of the soul, which had before prevailed. And although in a few weeks, this dispute in a great measure, subsided, yet the revival never recovered its former life and power. And there has appeared to be very few new instances of conviction or conversion since that time. This shows the pernicious tendency of such controversies to check religious awakenings, and quench the Spirit of God. How cautious, then, should all be of introducing such disputes in times of peculiar attention to divine things. . . . . . . But to proceed in the narration— It may be observed that most who have had a thorough conviction of their entire depravity, great guilt and danger, entertain a hope that they have become reconciled to God. A few yet remain under serious impressions, who do not suppose they have embraced the Saviour; while some, it is to be feared, who have been in some measure awakened to a sense of their sin and danger, have lost their conviction. . . . . . . There has appeared among those who were seriously affected, a peculiar disposition to hear, and get divine instruction, and an unwillingness to leave religious meetings after the public exercises were concluded, as long as they could hear religious conversation. It was pleasing to see with what solemn attention and apparent satisfaction, many of the youth listened to divine instruction, who a few weeks before, were thoughtless of the important concerns of religion, and took their greatest pleasure in balls, vain company and amusements. But the ball chambers, and the card-tables were now forsaken. And those who were serious, were deeply impressed with a sense of the hurtful tendency of such things to divert attention from divine things, quench the strivings of God's Spirit, and harden the heart.

One hundred have made a profession, and been received into this church since the revival began, of whom sixty-one are females, and thirty-nine males. About sixty are under thirty years of age, and there may be, perhaps, twelve that are nearly fifty or upwards. This shows the great importance of cordially engaging in religion in the season of youth. Most of those who have made a public profession suppose that they have become reconciled during this peculiar effusion of the Holy Spirit; but some, who date their conversion several years back, have now been more quickened and confirmed in their hopes. Others have been shaken from their old hopes, been brought to see that they were building on the sand, and have now hopefully embraced the Saviour, and thus built on the rock of ages. There are, perhaps, twenty who entertain a hope of having made their peace with God, that have not yet made a public profession of religion.

It may be remarked, that the converts are chiefly from families where one or both the parents were professors, or hopefully pious. This consideration affords parents a very powerful motive to engage in religion, and to bring up their children in the nurture and admonition of the Lord. By neglecting these things, parents are destroying both themselves, and their children.

Having given this general sketch of the beginning and progress of the revival, I shall proceed to some observations to illustrate in a more particular manner, the nature of the work.

It has been remarkably free from all irregularity and enthusiasm. The convictions have been rational, but deep and powerful. When first awakened, persons were generally moved by a sense of danger. They generally set out with a resolution, and the expectation of doing something to make themselves better—commend themselves to God, and procure his favor, having no just sense of their entire depravity of heart, or moral inability. But the more they attended to the duties of religion, and endeavored to make themselves better, the more sensible they became of their exceeding depravity and guilt.

Like the woman, who spent all she had to be healed of the physicians, they were sensible that they were nothing bettered, but rather grew worse. They were soon brought to see that their hearts were full of sin and opposition to God. When under thorough conviction, they would readily acknowledge that they were sensible that they were greatly opposed to God's character, laws and government—that they had always acted from a wicked, selfish heart, and therefore had never done any thing right in the sight of God. They would observe that they formerly had no idea that they were opposed to God, but used to suppose, that they had some love to him, and did many things which were right and acceptable to him, and that it therefore appeared as if it would be hard and unjust in God to doom them to destruction; but that they were now sensible that they had always been opposed to God—had always acted from a sinful temper, and so had been sinning against him in all their moral conduct, and that he might justly cast them off forever. In this stage of their convictions, they did not feel that their great sinfulness consisted in any particular sinful misconduct, or immorality, but in their hearts, that great fountain and source of all wickedness, and in the general temper which actuated them in all their conduct. They were feelingly convinced that they never could enjoy any real peace or happiness, or participate in the holy enjoyments of heaven, unless their hearts were renewed by the divine Spirit. They were also fully sensible, that such was their depravity and opposition to God, and holiness, that they never should repent, and cordially embrace the gospel, unless influenced by the Spirit of God; and that he might, in justice, leave them to go on and perish in their sins. Thus they felt that they lay at the mere sovereign, uncovenated mercy—that their only ground of hope was that God through Christ, would have mercy on whom he would have mercy. In this situation they were sensible, that the doctrine of divine sovereignty or election, which mankind naturally oppose, and deny with such bitterness, was their only ground of hope. For if God were not to have mercy upon them, till they had done something to recommend themselves to his mercy, or to procure his grace, they felt that their case would be hopeless. Neither did they feel that their hearts being wholly depraved or opposed to God, would afford them any just excuse for remaining impenitent; but they were feelingly convinced that should they perish, the blame would fall upon themselves. This view of their character and condition, stripped them of their self-righteousness, and self-dependence, rendered them sensible of their need of the Lord Jesus as their Saviour to deliver them both from the power and punishment of sin, and so prepared them to trust in him alone for salvation.

These were generally the views and feelings of those who now hope they are reconciled, while they were under conviction, although there might be some circumstantial differences. The convictions of some were more sharp and powerful than those of others. Some experienced them for a longer, some for a shorter term. But when they were very powerful, the subjects of them commonly found relief the sooner. A certain person who is among the hopeful converts, was not under real conviction more than half a day before her mind was filled with comfort. She lived in a remote part of the society, which rendered it difficult for her to attend public worship, and so had not been at any religious meetings since the uncommon attention began. But hearing of it, and of the conversation of some youths, who appeared to be converts, it struck her mind that it must be something great and powerful to produce such a change in their feelings and conversation; and that therefore, conversion must be a great and important change. Soon after this, she attended a meeting one evening, and thought she never before heard such truths and exhortations as were delivered by the speaker. As he endeavored to show the importance of religion for support on a dying bed, and preparation to meet our Judge in peace, she was affected with a sense of the dreadfulness of being called to meet death while in a state of sin and opposition against the Almighty. These thoughts lay with weight on her mind that night, till she fell asleep, and returned next morning when she awoke. But soon after she was very powerfully impressed with a sense of her exceeding wickedness, and felt as if she was the most vile, unworthy sinner on earth. She was so oppressed and disturbed with a sense of her sinfulness, that she could not attend to the concerns of her family. But before noon her mind was relieved. Her heart was filled with joy, love and praise to God, from a view of the loveliness of his glorious character, and of great mercy and condescension to sinners. Her great desire was, that all would praise God. She continued in this state, praising and rejoicing in God two or three days, before she thought she had any title to salvation.

Others were under conviction three or four days, or a week, and some for several weeks or months, before they appeared to become reconciled to God.

When they found sensible relief in their minds, it was commonly from a discovery of the glory, amiableness, and rectitude of the divine character, and from a disposition to submit to God. On discovering the glory of the divine character, they felt a disposition to love, praise, and rejoice in God, whatever became of them. They had new views and feelings towards almost every thing around them. Jesus Christ appeared glorious and lovely, and such an all-sufficient Saviour, as they needed; and therefore, they cordially trusted in him for salvation. They were pleased with the terms of the gospel, which are suited to exalt God, and humble sinners. They could rejoice that the Lord reigned, and that he would dispose of all events, as he saw best. The Bible appeared new and delightful. They cordially approved of its truths and requirements as just and reasonable. Sin appeared hateful. They felt themselves to be vile, and wondered that they had been spared, or that there was any hope in their case. They felt a disposition to love and forgive their enemies, and to seek and pray for the salvation of all around them. These and other similar views and feelings have been generally manifested by the converts. But some have manifested a much more lively sense of these things than others. At first their minds were so much engrossed by these objects, that they thought little or nothing about their own salvation. Others have observed that it seemed to them that God's character would appear glorious and lovely, and they could rejoice in it, even if they should be cast off. Their love to God and his government appeared to originate from a reconciliation to his holy character, and therefore to be essentially different from that false, selfish love, which arises from a belief that God is reconciled to us, and designs to save us in particular. For it is from finding in themselves this love and reconciliation to God's character, law and government, and a disposition to delight in the truths and duties of religion, that they indulge a hope, that they have become heirs of salvation.

Those who entertain this hope, generally appear to have a humble sense of their sinfulness, unworthiness, and entire dependence upon God, and continual need of the quickening, assisting influences of the Holy Spirit, and express an earnest desire to be freed from their remaining depravity. Numbers of the youth have observed, that they formerly supposed religion to be gloomy, and disagreeable, and that it would destroy all their pleasure and comfort, should they embrace it. Therefore, they could not think of engaging in it, and were really afraid they should have it. But they now say, they never knew what real peace or happiness was before—that at times, they find a joy and satisfaction in God and divine things, which far exceeds all the pleasures that the world can afford, and that they have experienced more real happiness in attending one religious meeting, than in all their vain and sinful amusements.

The peculiar doctrines of the gospel, such as the entire depravity of the natural heart, regeneration by the efficacious influences of the Holy Spirit, justification by faith alone, God's sovereignty and universal government, or his decrees and election—these doctrines which are so crossing to the feelings of the natural heart, and so bitterly opposed and denied by many, appear to be very fully and cordially embraced by those who are hopefully renewed. Although many of them once disliked these doctrines, and thought them very hard and unreasonable, as impenitent sinners generally do, yet they appeared to be led immediately into them by the convictions of the divine Spirit, as being the only doctrines, which afforded any ground of hope to sinners. Some of them have observed, that it appears to them, that every one who has been brought to a just sense of his condition, through the renewing influences of the Spirit, and become reconciled to God, must be convinced of the truth of these doctrines, and cordially embrace them.

It may be useful here to give some particular account of a remarkable display of the sovereign power and mercy of God in awakening a certain person. He was a young married man who was inclining to infidelity, and who made very light of the revival when it began, calling it delusion, enthusiasm and priestcraft. As his wife was among the first who became seriously impressed, he endeavored to divert and hinder her attention, and to ridicule her out of her seriousness. He was highly displeased because she was affected and shed tears at hearing a sermon, and he said he was ashamed of her folly, and that no preaching or minister could ever fetch a tear from his eye. Sometime after his wife was apparently reconciled to God, she was about to go with a number of others to be examined for admission into the church. He endeavored to dissuade her from it, saying that it was unnecessary, and that she could as well live religion without making a public profession, as with. But as she, thinking it to be her duty, went to be examined, he was greatly displeased—would hardly speak to her, and scarcely take his food for several days. He told her brother, that he designed to go to sea, and swore that he would never go into the meeting-house with her again. But that very day, there was a lecture appointed at the meeting-house, and as the family were getting ready to go, her father with whom he lived, proposed that he should go with them in the wagon. Forgetting his promise, he went, and as he entered the meeting-house, he was first of all powerfully struck with the recollection that he had sworn never to go there with his wife again. He was greatly shocked at the thought of his rash and wicked oath. The sermons which were delivered, made a deep and powerful impression on his mind. It seemed, he observed, as if the discourses were addressed directly to him, and he was greatly affected, and in tears, during a considerable part of the religious exercises. He was apparently in great distress of mind for some time, and seemed deeply sensible of the madness and wickedness of his former conduct, in opposing and making light of divine things. After a while he was relieved from his distress of mind, and obtained a hope that he was reconciled to God. He has since, with his wife, made a public profession of that religion, which he once opposed and despised. It is to be hoped that his life may be such as to adorn his Christian profession, and be evidential of a real change of heart. But whether it should be so or not, still it appears to have been a remarkable display of the power of God in favor of divine truth.

Such remarkable revivals of religion afford strong evidence that the Scriptures are from God, since the truths contained in them, are attended with such a divine power in awakening, reforming, and renewing sinners. No other doctrines, or schemes of religion have such powerful effects. The Bible informs us that the preaching of the gospel produced such happy and glorious effects, when it was first propagated by the apostles. Great multitudes both of Jews and Gentiles were then awakened, turned from sin to holiness, called out of darkness into marvelous light, and added to the church of Christ. When, therefore, we see the gospel now producing such effects, they greatly confirm its truth and divine origin.

Such seasons of peculiar attention to divine

things plainly manifest that the power which renders the gospel successful, is of God, and not of man, and that agreeably to the declaration of the apostle, "I have planted, Apollos watered, but God gave the increase." We see from facts, that at one time, the preaching of the gospel has little or no effect. Few or none are awakened and renewed. At another time, these same truths, which have been heard year after year with no apparent effect, are clothed with power, arrest the attention of numbers, and are the means of producing a wonderful change in their feelings and sentiments; so that many now cordially believe and embrace those truths, which a few weeks before, they bitterly opposed and denied; and now take pleasure in prayer, reading the Scriptures, serious conversation, and the other duties of religion, which but a short time since, they perhaps ridiculed and despised, or at least neglected and considered as very tedious and irksome. Such facts fully evince, that the power which produces these remarkable effects, is not of man, nor in the gospel itself, but of God.

The Sovereignty of God in the dispensations of his grace, is clearly displayed in such revivals; for it is then evident from facts that God has mercy on whom he will have mercy,—awakens and renews one, and not another, as he, in infinite wisdom, sees fit. Although, as before noticed, the hopeful converts are chiefly from families, where the Sabbath, public worship, and divine things have been regarded and reverenced; yet some have been under powerful impressions and convictions, who to human appearance, were as unlikely to be impressed, as almost any in the society. From the same family, some have been taken, and others have been left.

Persons who oppose, and make light of such peculiar revivals of religion, give the strongest evidence that they have never experienced the renewing influences of the divine Spirit.

Finally—in such seasons of uncommon attention to divine things, and among such a number of apparent converts, it is to be feared and expected that some are deceived, and will prove stony ground hearers, whose religion will endure but for a time; and that after a while they will fall away, and manifest by their conduct that they were building upon a foundation of sand. Should this be the case, although it would be very painful to the friends of religion, yet it would be no more, than what from Scripture and past experience, we have reason to fear; and therefore would afford no just objection against its being in general the work of the Lord. Since there is danger that some may turn back, and fall short of salvation, the apostolic directions appear very necessary, and applicable to those who now hope that they are the heirs of salvation. "Let him that thinketh he standeth, take heed lest he fall." "Take heed, brethren, lest there be in any of you an evil heart of unbelief in departing from the living God." As they regard the honor of religion, and their own eternal safety, it behooveth them to give all diligence to grow in grace, and make their calling and election sure. And we pray God that they may, in all things, adorn the doctrine of God, their Saviour, by a holy life—be found faithful in the cause of God until death, and then receive a crown of life.

CHAPTER XIV.

An account of a Revival of Religion in BURLINGTON, CONN., in the year 1799. By the Rev. JONATHAN MILLER.

THE unusual attention to religion in this small parish, became visible a little before the middle of February, 1799; though for several Sabbaths before that time, some greater degree of solemnity appeared on the congregation, than had been common, and a few religious conferences were attended. . . . . . . Undoubtedly in the beginning of the work, numbers were moved with little more than a sympathetic affection, arising from the novelty and seriousness of the impressive scene. But this was not in vain, for the Lord made use of it to open their ears to instruction; and as that subsided, it was in many instances followed by the most rational conviction of gospel truths, and a realizing sense of their importance, which have apparently produced the most happy effects. Numbers who were unmoved at first, have since been made to inquire with earnestness, what they shall do to be saved. And convictions, I think, gradually increased through the following spring and summer. I have conversed with between forty and fifty who have received comfort, and appear to be reconciled to God. Many others are yet attentive, while there is reason to fear that the seriousness of some is on the decline, if not altogether at an end. Although there has been a great variety in the dealings of God with different individuals who now give reason to hope that they are heartily reconciled to him, with respect to the length, degree, and distinct quality of their convictions, and the strength and bitterness of their sensible heart-risings against God, in the course of their convictions, and the clearness of their views, and greatness of their joys, when they were at first reconciled, yet there is a general similarity in the accounts which they all, or nearly all, have given of themselves. They have at first, generally, though not universally, been principally affected with a sense of their danger of the wrath of God, and all have resorted to their own works, to conciliate his favor, without that submission to him and reliance on Christ which the gospel requires. While pursuing this course, their painful apprehensions of divine wrath, have been gradually overbalanced by successive and increasing discoveries of their guilt and obstinate depravity of heart, until they have felt their entire dependence on the sovereign mercy of God to renew their hearts. While in this situation, they have generally been sensible of dreadful heart-risings against God and his government. Some have related their feelings while in this situation, which were too dreadful to be repeated. Several have been on the borders of despair. They who have received comfort, look back on this, as the season of their greatest distress of soul, and it has often been so great, as very much to interrupt, and sometimes wholly to destroy their sleep, labor, and appetite for food. After continuing for some time in this state, oppressed with a sense of their desperate wickedness, many of them have been suddenly relieved from the anguish of their souls. Of these some have been immediately filled with great joy, and admiring views of the excellencies and perfections of God. Every thing about them, even the natural creation, has appeared new, because declarative of the presence and agency of God, which they had never before regarded in this light. Others have, at first, only experienced a calm composure of mind, in which, without any sensible heart-risings against God, they have attentively contemplated his character and government—their own extreme vileness, and his sovereignty in the dispensations of his grace. They have seen and acknowledged the justice and fitness of his administrations, felt themselves wholly at his disposal, and consented that it should be so; but at the same time, had no sensible exercises or effusions of love, joy, or praise, and did not view themselves entitled to the promises of the gospel; but even found that they were losing their convictions. This state of mind has generally been followed in a few hours, or a few days, by an admiring sense of the excellency and glory of God, and a spirit of praise, love and comfort in him; sometimes excited by discoveries of Christ, and the glory of his work of redemption, and the fullness and sufficiency of his salvation; and at other times, by a view of the divine law, and the other various manifestations which God has made of his perfections. These exercises have suggested to their minds a hope that they are now born of God. Of this, however, none have appeared very confident at first; but their hopes have been expressed with caution, and have often been feeble and intermitting. As their religious exercises have been, by turns, more or less fervent, and, in their view, productive of obedience, their hopes have increased or diminished.

Many of them have observed, that the happiness which they have possessed in religious exercises, in respect to purity and sublimity, greatly exceeds all the sinful pleasures that they ever enjoyed. They appear to delight exceedingly in God, and their religion is to them a refreshing feast.

A number of those whose exercises have been here described, were formerly opposed to the doctrines of God's decrees, and particular election; but are now without exception convinced of their truth and importance, and of the total depravity of the natural heart. Two or three were inclined to universalism, but have now abandoned those opinions, and view them as false and pernicious. One, in particular, was a confirmed universalist, and had been so for some years. He is a man about forty years of age, of a determined spirit, disposed to be confident in his own opinion, and to give little heed to the opinions of others in matters of religion. I shall here give an abstract of the account which he gave me of himself.

"I was," said he, "a real universalist, and fully believed those sentiments. After the awakening began, I had some conversation with a religious neighbor on the subject, and left him with a sensible inquietude on my mind.

I went home, took my Bible for relief, and turned to those texts which I had long considered as full proof of my sentiments; but on carefully reading and considering them, they did not appear so conclusive as they had done. I knew that I had no religion myself, and I determined that I would now attend to it, and repent, and believe on Christ, which I conceived could be easily accomplished, so that I might be safe, even though my sentiments concerning the salvation of all men, should not prove true. I set about the work, but in a few days relapsed into my old careless habits. A reflection on this gave me some alarm, and I resolved and entered on the business again and again, but to no better effect than before; until, at length, I felt in some measure my dependence on God to enable me to keep my resolutions. All this time, my confidence in universalism gradually grew weaker. I had now had much anxiety and concern of mind for several weeks, but remained opposed to the doctrines of the entire depravity of the carnal heart, divine sovereignty and election, till, on a certain day, I was alone on some business at a distance from my house, God discovered to me my own heart to that degree, that for a considerable time I can have no recollection of any circumstance or object about me. My attention was so entirely swallowed up by the dreadful discoveries of my own heart, that I know of nothing else which passed in my mind, until, at length, I found myself prostrate on the earth. I left the business, on which I went out, undone, and returned home with a heavy load on my mind, and was unable to do any business for several days. I got no relief, until, feeling my absolute dependence on the sovereign will of God to dispose of me as he should see fit, I resigned myself into his hands, sensible that if he should renew me, I should be saved; but if not, and if he should send me to hell, he would be perfectly just, and I should see it and know it forever."

It was some days after this, and after he gave me this account of himself, that he first began to entertain a hope that he was interested in the promises of the gospel, though he had much comfort when he gave me this relation, and had set up the worship of God in his family, which till this time, he had always neglected; and he had taken pains to convince one whom he had led into the persuasion that all men will be saved, and has since visited others for the same purpose. But whether his conversion be genuine, must remain to be proved by its fruits, and perseverance in religion.

To the account given of this man, I will subjoin that of another—a man about fifty-six years of age, who had no great share of general information, or sociability. He had been very inattentive to religion, even in speculation, and had very much neglected public worship. When the awakening first began among us, this man had let himself out at work, in a neighboring town, but after two or three months he returned. He observed the great alteration that had taken place among the people, and was led by it to reflect on his own sinful and miserable condition, and became deeply impressed with a sense of his danger. From this time he constantly attended religious meetings, and soon acquired some just views of the state of the controversy between God and himself, and expressed his views with much feeling and propriety. Not long after, he manifested a spirit of submission to God. He was then asked whether he was willing that God should govern all things, according to his own good pleasure? He readily answered, "Yes, this is what I want." It was replied, perhaps, if he should, he would cut you off. He answered, "Well, I won't find fault with him if he does. I won't say, I submit, and then find fault with him because he does not do with me as I wish he would." He said these things with an emphasis and expression which cannot be copied, and which apparently bespoke the feelings of his heart. He remained for several weeks rejoicing in God, and in his government, and in the doctrines and duties of the gospel. His countenance was cheerful, and even his natural abilities, especially for free, social conversation, seemed to be enlarged, although at the time he had no idea he was a real Christian, or was entitled to the promises. His serious neighbors, indeed, considered him as one born again; and one of them supposing by the tenor of his conversation on religious subjects, that doubtless he considered himself a convert, requested him to state the reasons which made him suppose or hope that he was a Christian. He replied, "I don't think I am one—I have no idea I am; but I hope I shall be." Mention was made to him of the gracious promises which God had made to such as would cast themselves upon his mercy. He answered, "I choose that he should do with me as he thinks fit." Since that time, by comparing his exercises with the Word of God, he has conceived a humble hope that he has real religion; and he continues to possess much joy and comfort, at the same time that a sense of his own vileness and unworthiness increases upon him. But he now says, that a sense of his vileness neither interrupts his happiness, nor leads him to dread the day of judgment, for his hope is Christ alone.

CHAPTER XV.

An account of a Revival of Religion in Avon, Conn., in the year 1799. By the Rev. Rufus Hawley.

On the eighth of March, 1799, some young people sent to me, requesting that I would attend a conference the ensuing evening. I attended, and found a considerable number of people collected, of various ages. We prayed, and attended to the important truths of the gospel. It was evident that some minds were impressed. The Sabbath evening following, there was a conference attended. Many people were present. The meeting was solemn.

The next Tuesday, a number of ministers came, and a lecture was attended at the meeting-house, and in the evening another, at my house. The people appeared anxious to hear the Word. The day following, a sermon was delivered at another house, when a large number of people were gathered together, and appeared more attentive than usual. It began to be evident about this time that the Lord was with us of a truth. Some began to be alarmed, and to inquire what they should do to be saved. The next Monday, (March 25,) a neighboring minister preached in the day-time, and another in the evening, to a crowded and listening assembly. In April, the religious attention increased greatly. New instances of conviction were frequent, and some began to obtain comfort and hope. In some instances, the people attended six or seven sermons a week. Old, middle aged, and young people, were the subjects of God's work. There was now a great shaking among the dry bones. Conferences were set up in every part of the parish. Balls, all merry meetings and public diversions were laid aside, and the people were more engaged to attend religious meetings, than they had been heretofore for carnal diversions. People of all ages, from fifteen to upwards of sixty, were deeply impressed. The distress of some was so great, that it deprived them in a great measure of their food and sleep, for a season. Many confessed their sins, complained of the hardness of their hearts, the abounding wickedness of their lives, and appeared very sensibly to feel that it would be just in God to cast them off forever. And every person who, in a judgment of charity, is a subject of the regenerating power of the divine Spirit, appears full in the belief of the divine sovereignty, decrees, election, and all the essential doctrines of the gospel.

A young man who had obtained a hope that he was a subject of the new birth, said he might be deceived with regard to the state of his soul, and perish at last; but he believed God would do right, and he was willing to be at his disposal. Others have expressed themselves in much the same manner. Free grace, and the atonement and merits of Christ, are extolled by those who are the subjects of a change of heart. Numbers, at times, have such nearness to, and communion with God, that they have great foretastes of heaven, and joy unspeakable.

At a conference one evening, a man being asked if he found any happiness in religion, replied, " Yes; since I have been attending the present meeting, and uniting with the people of God, in worshiping him, I have enjoyed more real happiness in religion, than ever I enjoyed in all other things, through my whole past life." All the mirth and carnal pleasures in the world, he said, were nothing, compared with the sweets of true religion. Some others were asked the same question, who said that what had been observed, corresponded with their real feelings. They now found by their own experience, that "wisdom's ways are ways of pleasantness, and all her paths are peace."

A considerable number who, in times past, did not pray in their families, have now set up family religion, and are constant, and to appearance devout, in their performance of this duty. And those who heretofore did not worship God in their houses, now plead fervently with God, that there may be no prayerless families. In this small society, there are thirty or forty men who pray at conferences, not only in my absence, but most of them, (upon being requested,) when I am present. Some, who years ago had openly violated the laws of Christ, and purposed never to confess their faults, have freely made a public confession of their sins against the Most High; and have said, that although it was what their hearts once totally opposed, yet now they could do it, as freely as ever they did any thing in their lives. Now they see and feel the past stubbornness of their wills, and the hardness of their hearts. And their sins being set in order before their eyes, and their wills bowed, they acknowledge with the penitent psalmist, "Against thee, thee only, have I sinned, and done this evil in thy sight." And they plead, "Have mercy upon me, O God, according to thy loving kindness; according unto the multitude of thy tender mercies, blot out our transgressions. Wash us thoroughly from our iniquity, and cleanse us from our sins."

Some persons, when they have come to converse upon entering into covenant, and joining with the church, have said they did not think, in time past, they should ever have any desire to join with the church, and partake of the Lord's supper—they did not think they should desire to have so much concern with religion; but now they wished to be joined to the visible family of God, and had earnest longings of mind to commemorate the dying love of the dear Redeemer.

The work of God, in this parish, has not been so great as in some other places; yet considering the smallness of the society, which consists of but little more than one hundred families, it must be confessed the work is truly glorious. There is reason to hope and believe many persons will remember this happy day, with joy and praise, not only whilst they live, but through eternity.

Through the whole awakening, it has been most evident that the work was the effect of the divine Spirit. It has been peculiarly free from noisy, blind zeal and frenzy. The convictions of sinners have been solemn and pungent; and there is reason to hope that a considerable number have been born of the Spirit.

Since the awakening began among my people, between forty and fifty have made a profession of religion, and joined the church. Those who have long been in Christ, appear to have had fresh anointings of the divine Spirit, and to have been stirred up to pray more fervently than usual for themselves and for the prosperity of Zion. Those who were in Christ before, and likewise those who have lately professed faith in him, have, in general, exhibited a good degree of evidence that they are joined to the Lord, and have his Spirit. They delight in the duties of religion. The service of God is now sweet and pleasant to them, in all its branches. They love to read God's Word. Many have said the Bible is entirely a new book to them. The perusal of it, which afforded them no satisfaction before, now yields them the highest delight. Now they search the Scriptures daily, and say with the psalmist, "O how love I thy law; it is daily my delight." Those that rarely came to the house of God, are constant attendants. They love the sanctuary of God, the place where his honor dwelleth, and delight in the ordinances of the gospel. Their soul is satisfied as with marrow and fatness, and they praise God with joyful lips.

But we fear that some who profess to hope that they have now made their peace with God, will so apostatize from their profession, that it will appear that their religion is like the morning cloud and the early dew, which soon goeth away; though we are ready to hope better things of them, and things that accompany salvation. And notwithstanding the prospects have been so promising, and the minds of nearly all the people were turned upon religious subjects, yet at present we have reason to fear that the attention of many has declined, and that many are still dead in trespasses and sins. We fear they will finally perish, and their condemnation, in that case, will be awfully aggravated by the uncommon and powerful means which God has now been using with them. How dreadful, after having been exalted to heaven, to be thrust down to hell!

CHAPTER XVI.

An account of a Revival of Religion in the town of Bloomfield, Conn., in the year 1799. By the Rev. William F. Miller.

Previous to this uncommon seriousness which there has been among us, the cause of religion for many years had been in a low and declining state. In the month of February, 1799, I appointed a weekly conference, believing that the prevailing wickedness of the day called for extraordinary prayer to God. In the latter part of March, and the beginning of April, there appeared the small beginnings of more than ordinary attention to the things of God's kingdom. Some were struck with a deep conviction of their sin and danger, and others were alarmed. This attention to religion continued to increase for several weeks, till it had become so general in the parish, that it was judged expedient to set up, in various parts of the society, several religious meetings. From this time, the house of God was filled on the Sabbath, and these weekly meetings in various parts of the parish were attended by from two hundred and fifty to three and four hundred people. No pains were spared to hear the gospel preached. All was solemn. There was no noise, or enthusiasm. Many might be seen, from time to time, melted into tears, from the impressive force of divine truth, set home upon their hearts, by a divine influence. They were convinced that they were truly wretched, and miserable, and unholy in the sight of God. They saw that they were, and always had been, the enemies of God. They had such a sense of the depravity of their hearts, as to be convinced that no power was sufficient to change them but the Almighty power of God. These convictions of soul made them sensible, that however much their hearts had been opposed to the doctrines of divine sovereignty, total depravity, and salvation by grace, yet they were thus depraved in heart, and that it was wholly in vain to hope for salvation in any other way. They now saw that if they were saved at all, it would be owing to the sovereign mercy of God. In the midst of these distressing fears and sorrows of soul, in many instances they were at once relieved by an instantaneous change of their views, when a new apprehension of the character of God, or of Christ, broke in upon their minds in a most sweet and glorious manner, in consequence of which they felt their enmity and opposition to the character of God, and of the Lord Jesus Christ, to the law and the gospel, taken away; and they beheld such purity and goodness—such sweetness, beauty and glory in divine things, as filled their hearts with unspeakable joy. Overpowered with the greatness of the change, under the view which they then had of God and religion, they cried out, " What have we been about, that we have not been praising God before ? O, we never knew what happiness is, till now."

Hitherto, among the hopeful converts, there has appeared a great uniformity in the prevailing temper of their minds. It has been evident that whosoever is born of God, loveth God, and Christ, and the law, and the gospel, and divine institutions. They continue to manifest a desire after the sincere milk of the word, to grow thereby in grace and knowledge; an attachment to the Holy Scriptures, and to gospel institutions; and an exemplary walk and conversation.

The particular experiences of the following individuals, may serve to illustrate the nature of the work.

A young woman, who for several weeks had been considerably awakened and alarmed, and who by strong temptations had been induced to strive against the convictions of her mind, was at length pricked in the heart with such distress, as compelled her in earnest to ask the way of salvation. She now reviewed her past life with a soul filled with horror. Her prayerless life—her many misspent Sabbaths—her former wrong motives in attending upon public worship, the prevailing wickedness of her heart, filled her with keen remorse. Lamenting her former mis-improvement of the Sabbath, she said, " I now wish for the return of the Sabbath more than I ever did for any amusement."— Thus impressed, she embraced all opportunities of public and private instruction, while her convictions increased. At length, hearing a sermon from these words, " What meanest thou, O sleeper? Arise, call upon thy God," she was much affected with a sense that she had been no more awakened to call upon God for his pardoning mercy. Sleep fled from her eyes, and her soul was most of the night lifted up in cries to God. She continued in this state of distress about a fortnight. She had thought her preceding convictions as great as nature could endure; but now she found they were not to be compared with the present agonies of her soul. It seemed that nature must sink under the heavy burden, while she felt the weight of her guilt before God. In this distress, one day, while at prayer, her mind appeared to undergo a change, which was followed with such a delightful view of the holiness, justice and goodness of God, as filled her soul with unspeakable love to him, and brought her, as she hoped, to resign herself wholly to his sovereign disposal. Upon this ravishing view of the holiness and justice of God, which broke in upon her soul, till then unsubdued, without thinking of its being a regenerating change, "In a moment," she said, "the heavy load in my breast was removed. A sweet peace filled my soul. I burst out in rapture, I will forever bow and resign myself up to thee, a sinner as I am! O, I have need to be humbled before thee! I have need to confess my sins to thee, and to be low before thee, guilty and vile as I am. But while thus humble and vile in my own eyes, my soul was filled with unspeakable joy—with such happiness as I never before experienced. My heart was filled with love and gratitude to God. I felt an unspeakable delight in him. It seemed to me that I never could sufficiently praise him. This was the happiest day of my life. O, I never knew what happiness was before." The same day, greatly affected with what she had now experienced, she rode to see one of her sisters who lived several miles distant; and, as she rode, her mind was wholly engrossed with religion, and she relates, "It seemed to me that I enjoyed more happiness in half an hour, than I had ever enjoyed in my whole life before. The goodness and mercy of God, and the sufferings of Christ for sinners, were a feast to my soul. I was happy to be alone. I felt humbled and unworthy, but I saw a sufficiency in Christ, and felt that all the glory belonged to God."

The experience of another woman, about thirty years of age, was as follows: For several years, she had rarely attended public worship any where. But she was now aroused to attend to divine things, by hearing much said about the present revival of religion in the parish—by seeing her sister under conviction, and hearing her converse upon religion; and by a lecture which she had attended in the neighborhood, and which had been set up after the commencement of the revival. For a few weeks, she kept her convictions wholly to herself. She was afraid to be seen reading the Bible, or to have it known that she was concerned for the salvation of her soul, lest she should be derided or be thought to pretend to more religion than other people. To hide her convictions from the eyes of the world, she spent all her spare time in a chamber by herself, in reading the Bible, and in prayer to God. For this purpose, she set up late at night, and rose at daylight in the morning. But the power of conviction increasing, her distress compelled her to ask for instruction and counsel. And although greatly burdened at the time, yet, after hearing the great doctrines of the gospel explained, she went away more sorrowful than she came. The evening following, she was struck with a still deeper sense of the greatness of her sins, and of the dreadful wrath of God revealed from heaven against the ungodly, upon hearing a sermon from these words, Rom. 3 : 19, " Now we know that what things soever the law saith, it saith to them that are under the law ; that every mouth may be stopped, and all the world may become guilty before God." " While hearing this sermon," she says, " it seemed to me just as though I stood before the judgment seat of Christ. I felt like a criminal. I never before had such an awful sense of the guilt of my sins, though my distresses had been very great. My mouth was stopped, and I had nothing to say for myself. Such was the agony of my soul, that I slept but little that night. The next day and night, and the following forenoon, I spent chiefly in prayer to God and in reading the Bible. As I read 2 Cor. 5: 17, 'Therefore, if any man be in Christ, he is a new creature; old things are passed away, behold all things are become new,' my mind was, in a most surprising manner, brought to submit to God, and suddenly impressed with a delightful view of his great goodness and forgiving mercy, through the Lord Jesus Christ. My troubled soul was strangely eased of its sorrows. For a few minutes, a sweet calm, and a resignation to God's will followed, till my mind was filled with inexpressible joy and rejoicing in God. It now seemed to me, that I could not refrain from praising God aloud. I longed to be by myself, away from every body. I laid down the Bible, and went out into the field, speaking the praises of God; and there every thing around me seemed to be praising him. I now saw his goodness in the spires of grass before me—in the trees—in the birds—in the heavens—in the shining sun—in the earth —in its abounding fullness of every thing for the use of man,—and above all, in his long forbearance to such a sinner as I had been. I seemed to be in a new world, so different did every thing now appear, as flowing from the goodness of God. For now his goodness appeared in every thing. O, how could I sin as I have done against a God of such infinite goodness? It seemed that God and Christ could never be sufficiently praised. I now wanted to have every body praise them. It seemed strange that my eyes had never been opened before. I now wondered how any body could live without praising God. O, how vile I felt before God, as a sinner, dreadfully guilty and unworthy of his notice; and yet I felt unspeakably happy in praising him, as a holy and righteous God."

This person, for nearly a year, has lived in a high state of religious enjoyment. She spends considerable time daily in reading the Bible and in prayer. She visits the sick with peculiar tenderness; and, at times, is greatly exercised for the salvation of others. Her distresses for the salvation of others have been so great, that she hardly knows how to account for them, while, in respect to herself, she feels so happy in the enjoyment of God. The Sabbath is her delight, and hearing the gospel her sweetest enjoyment.

A man, about sixty years of age, of respectable character, and a regular attendant on public worship, soon after this powerful work of God began among us, was convinced that it was a divine work, and was excited to a diligent use of the means of grace. His mind was struck with a conviction that outward morality would not save him from the condemning sentence of a broken law, though it is the dependence of too many—that in his past morality he had been so far from yielding an acceptable obedience to the law of God, that he stood before God condemned for innumerable transgressions. He felt himself to be a miserable sinner in the hands of a holy God. His forebodings of eternal misery, awakened by the divine Spirit, took away all peace from his mind, and filled him with great distress. He was now bowed down under a deep sense of his great guilt, and felt that nothing but a change of heart by the Holy Ghost, could prepare him for the kingdom of heaven. "While thus deeply distressed," he says, "one Sabbath morning, on my way to meeting, my heart appeared to undergo an instantaneous change, and I was suddenly overpowered with a most affecting sense of God's holiness and justice, which before I could never satisfactorily comprehend—of his readiness to pardon the penitent sinner—and of the glorious sufficiency there is in Christ. My views of divine things were all changed in a moment. I now saw that I had never before had any just sense of the righteousness of God, nor of the way of salvation by Christ. And though I felt vile in my own eyes, my soul was filled with unspeakable joy in God, and in the blessed Redeemer. I had thought that I before knew what happiness was; but the happiness I then enjoyed was of a different nature, and not to be compared with what I now felt, from the soul-satisfying view I had of Christ. A sense of what Christ had done for sinners, while it laid me in the dust, filled my heart with joy and praise. I had, also, sometimes thought that I had a just sense of my littleness before God, when I compared myself with the smallest insect. But now I found my mistake, and said, that I had never before had any just apprehension of my nothingness and unworthiness before him. That was the happiest Sabbath and the happiest day of my life. My soul was filled with the sweetest joy and rejoicing in God, and Christ, and heavenly things."

I shall conclude this narrative of individuals, with an account of the experiences of another man, of forty-five years of age. This man was greatly awakened several weeks before he let it be known, as he had an opportunity of hearing the private instruction given to his wife, who was also under conviction. When he made known the state of his mind, he was told how wicked and inexcusable sinners are in delaying repentance—the necessity of regeneration—the sovereignty of God in it; and the importance of improving the present time to make his peace with God. His convictions increased for many weeks; and while some, who had been awakened long after him, were now rejoicing in hope, his anxiety continued. This greatly discouraged him, making him envious at those who had obtained a hope, and exciting in his mind hard thoughts of God. He was tempted to think at one time, that all his convictions were a delusion; at another time, that God was hard and unjust, that he had not noticed his prayers, while others were regenerated after less conviction than he had experienced; and at another time, to believe that all his prayers and seekings were in vain, and to desist from all further seekings, since God was a sovereign and unchangeable being. But by this resolution he could not abide. The power of God was too great for him; for his convictions returned with double force upon his mind. They compelled him to an earnest attendance on secret prayer—reading the Scriptures, and hearing the gospel, which affected his mind with a deep sense of the danger of living in sin to advanced life. "I now," said he, " saw the danger of abusing the calls of God in early life, lest we should be given over to hardness of heart in advanced age. I wished to warn all young people not to neglect the offers of mercy, as I had done, lest like me, when further advanced in life, they should cry and seek to God, and not be heard. For, it now seemed to me, that the reason why God had not heard me was, because I had lived so long in impenitence. I was particularly distressed in reflecting upon my past abuse of the Christian Sabbath, and neglect of the public worship of God, and wished to exhort both old and young, not to abuse these privileges as I had done. Instead of becoming better, or finding grace, as I had long expected, I now appeared to myself to grow more and more hardened in sin, and to be further than ever from the kingdom of God. O, my soul was filled with horror in reflecting upon my past abuse of divine mercies; and the danger of being left to be miserable forever, was so strongly impressed upon my mind, that it was almost insupportable."

Having one day told him of the comforting hope of his wife, I asked him how he could live any longer in impenitence, when so many were brought home to God, and now his wife in particular; reminding him that he must be sensible he was to blame for living in impenitence—that it was wrong to cast the guilt of his sins upon

God—and that the condemnation of the finally impenitent, after enjoying the privileges of the present day, would be peculiarly aggravated. He has since told me the effects of this conversation. "I never," said he, "felt so envious as I did when you told me of my wife's hope. I hated myself and every body else. And when you told me of my inexcusableness after all my strivings, I hated such discourse, while my conscience convinced me that it was right; for my distress now increased, and seemed to be more than I could live under. I had before felt as though I should sink under my convictions; but now I felt as though they would kill me, such appeared to be the dreadful hardness and wickedness of my heart. I was strongly tempted to put an end to my life, that I might get out of my present misery; but I instantly thought that this temptation must be from the devil, who was now uniting with my wicked heart to destroy me, and I resisted it with abhorrence, while a sense of having for a moment indulged such a wicked thought, covered me with shame and confusion. I could no longer find ease. That was a sleepless night. By reason of the horrors of my mind, I arose the next morning two or three hours before day, pained with dreadfully wicked and tormenting thoughts—with hard thoughts of God, and distressing thoughts of my own wretchedness. Such horror and misery were before me, that it seemed as if the very thoughts of them would take my life away. Full of despairing agony, I arose from my chair and went through the room where my Bible lay, and turning my eyes upon it, with hatred and malice I took it up to put it out of my sight forever, resolving to pay no more attention to it, for a moment giving myself up to utter despair. But in this conflict, my heart failed me. I returned to my chair again, and in unspeakable agony of soul, was now convinced of the dreadful enmity of my heart against God. I felt my helpless condition as a sinner, and saw that God only was able to change my heart. For about an hour I continued in earnest cries to God for mercy. I felt guilty and condemned, and that God would be just in punishing me with everlasting destruction, even though he were to save all the rest of mankind; being convinced that his mercies were his own, and that he had a right to bestow them on whom he pleased. My distress forced me to cry aloud, 'O, Lord Jesus, have mercy on me now, or I perish for ever. O, now I feel the need of Jesus!' My mind was immediately relieved. A sweet calm followed for about twenty-four hours, in which I felt a full resignation to the will of God, and a real abhorrence of all sin. And after this calm, the Christian Doxology was brought to mind with great power and sweetness. Hereupon my mind was filled with inexpressible joy and delight in the Trinity. I said to myself, 'what have I been about, that I have not been praising God before.' My joys continued to increase for about three weeks, while I felt a most lively sense of my own unworthiness in the sight of God, and of the all-sufficiency of his grace, through Jesus Christ, for pardon and salvation. I now seemed to feel sweetly resigned to the will of God in all things—in sickness, or in health, or in any other thing that God should see fit to bring upon me. I rejoiced that he was God, and just such a God as he is. This consideration, above all others, gave me inexpressible satisfaction in him. And I now found great delight in joining with my family in prayer, a duty which I had all my life neglected against the dictates of my conscience."

In the preceding account of individuals, I have, for the sake of brevity, confined myself to the convictions which preceded their comforts, and the holy exercises which immediately followed.

CHAPTER XVII.

An account of a Revival of Religion in MIDDLEBURY, CONN., in the years 1799 and 1800. By the Rev. IRA HART.

This society is but lately formed, and I am the first settled minister. I am informed that some years since, there was a small revival of religion, and that several persons were added to the church. At the time of my settlement, while every thing else appeared favorable, the spirit and power of vital piety seemed to be almost gone. There was a commendable and general punctuality in attending public worship on the Sabbath; but not that animation, that fixed, engaged attention and solemnity, which characterize those who tread the courts of the Lord, to be fed with the bread of life, and the waters of life. We had a number of praying families, but alas, too many in which the morning and evening sacrifice was not offered to God, and no supplication made by parents, for the gracious presence of the Redeemer with themselves and their children.

Several cases of discipline existed in the church, which required the tenderest management, and which lay upon the brethren as a heavy burden. All saw and acknowledged the evil, and longed to have it removed, but in the general inactivity and discouragement, and owing perhaps in some degree to the want of a settled minister, nothing effectual had been done. The church appeared timid, and some of the enemies of the cross exulted and cast reproach.

Returning home from some places where there was a revival, my mind became impressed with the idea that nothing so effectually kept off the divine blessing from us, as our neglect of those cases of discipline. The church were urged to proceed immediately, and being convinced that reformation must begin at the house of God, entered into the affair with spirit. In July a complaint was regularly exhibited, and a day for the trial appointed. A circumstance now took place, which showed that the Lord was with us. Though the accused, a man of about eighty years of age, appeared for some time not to regard the summons of the church, and though pains were taken to suppress the evidence, yet such was the power of God that he found no peace, till his heart melted, and he appeared and pleaded guilty to the complaint. His venerable appearance, his apparent deep-felt penitence and humility, rendered the scene peculiarly affecting to the church and to his own family. On his confession, which was public, he was restored to our charity and communion. It was indeed a solemn transaction, and seemed to interest the whole audience, and to make an impression highly favorable to religion.

Soon after, returning from a neighboring society, I called at his house. I perceived a stranger present, and a considerable alteration in the countenances of the family; but whether there was any thing special, or whether their feelings were unfavorably excited, on account of my conduct in the late affair of discipline, I knew not. Judge, then, my agreeable surprise, when soon called upon by the mother to answer to her daughter and the stranger, the great question, what must we do to be saved? To this uexpected question I gave the Scripture answer, and soon found they were indeed pricked in the heart. And here, the late awakening with which a merciful and sovereign God hath visited us, may be properly said to begin. It was soon found that other members of the same family were in a similar state of conviction. This interposition of God was too striking to pass unnoticed. It manifested to the church, and to all, that the way of duty is the way of safety, and the way in which divine blessings are usually dispensed. It served to rouse the friends of Zion. They awoke from discouragement and declension; and their hearts and mouths began to be open on the subject of religion. It was judged proper, although in the most busy season of the year, immediately to appoint occasional lectures. These were first preached at private houses, but the number of hearers soon made it necessary to attend in the meeting-house. These lectures were several of them preached by neighboring ministers, to whom we are greatly indebted for their kind instructions and labors of love. New cases of conviction soon occurred in different parts of the society. The still small voice of God, here and there spake to sundry careless and secure sinners, causing great distress of mind, and most anxious inquiry after the way of escape from the wrath to come. Our lectures were seriously and solemnly attended. The Sabbath was a solemn day. In private companies, and in the corners of the streets, religion was the theme of conversation. Professing Christians confessed, with tears, their short comings in duty, and the wound the blessed Redeemer had received in the house of his friends. They looked back with grief and wonder upon themselves, and melted with contrition before God. The aged and the young were agreed in saying, " it was never so seen in Israel." The call for religious instruction was now so great, that it became necessary, besides the lectures, to establish conferences, which were attended by numbers with great seriousness and profit.

As several of the first cases were among the youth, a serious opposition was on the eve of commencing among some of the young people, who objected to the religious attention of their companions as calculated to destroy their amusements. On these they were bent. Take these away, they could almost say with Micah, " Ye have taken away my gods, and what have I more?" A merciful God interposed, and taught them that the work was his own. They wisely desisted, that they might not be found fighting against God. One young man, on the appearance of the religious concern among the youth, began profanely to ridicule those who were under distress of mind. In the midst of his career, he attended public worship on the Sabbath, and as he entered the gallery, God met him and pierced him with a sharp arrow of conviction. He stumbled to a seat, and amid the horrors of a guilty, awakened conscience, sat trembling in view of truth and the awful iniquity of his heart; and soon after testified to the excellency of that Saviour, and that religion, which he before despised. This providence was, I believe, generally received by the youth as an admonition from heaven. They gave up their vain amusements, crowded to conferences and lectures, and a goodly number of them have, as we charitably hope, been brought from darkness to light. It was indeed a glorious season—a season which will long be remembered by many precious souls, as the time of their espousals to Christ.

At the close of the year, I found the number of persons seriously impressed to be about seventy. Some had already obtained a hope of cordial reconciliation to God, through Jesus Christ; but many others refused to submit themselves to Christ on the terms of the gospel. To the number above mentioned, who appeared to be under great distress of mind, may probably be added many others, who were more or less alarmed, as there was an almost general appearance of seriousness and alarm throughout the society.

The awakening has embraced persons of almost all ages, from fifteen to sixty-five. Of the forty-one who have been admitted to the church, seventeen were young people, six males and eleven females. Of the whole number, there are seventeen males, and twenty-four females. Excepting the seventeen young persons, the remainder are mostly young heads of families. This gives a hopeful prospect that the rising generation will more extensively enjoy the great blessings of family prayer and religious instruction. These blessings, it is hoped, will be more highly valued than they have been, for a greater part of the convictions and hopeful conversions among us have existed in families of prayer, and where one or both of the parents were professing Christians. The sovereignty of God has been eminently displayed in this revival. Not those whom we expected, but whom God pleased, he called to repentance. One is taken, and another left. Great exertions and pains were bestowed on some, who yet remain unconcerned; while upon another, a transient remark, or the occasional quotation of a text of Scripture, in the hands of God, became effectual unto conviction and salvation.

From what God has done for us, it is thought, all churches may learn the importance and safety of faithfully maintaining the discipline which Christ has established for the recovery of his erring children. If the discipline of the church is conducted with the prudence, vigilance, and brotherly love which the case requires, the blessing of God may be confidently expected.

It gives me unspeakable pleasure to mention the general good conduct of those, particularly the youths, who have made a public profession of religion. " By their fruits ye shall know them," is the maxim of Christ; and it is hoped that they will continue by exemplary lives to manifest to the world that they have been with Jesus, have imbibed his spirit, and are, like him, devoted to honor and glorify their Father in heaven.

I propose now to give some account of particular exercises of individuals.

I shall begin with the case of a young woman, a professor of religion, who had been induced to attend a place of amusement, which she afterwards became convinced was improper. The circumstances will be mentioned mostly in her own words, as communicated to me in a letter.

"In compliance with your request, I give you my opinion and experience of the impropriety of a professor's attending balls. Permit me, however, to relate some particulars in an earlier part of my life. At the age of thirteen, I was admitted into company as an equal with those of twenty and twenty-five. At sixteen, the Lord was pleased to stop my career of folly, and to call my mind from the world, by a deep sense of the importance of religion, to the present and future happiness of my soul. After a painful conviction of the awful depravity of my heart, the amazing distance I was at from God by nature, my desert of everlasting punishment, and the total inability of helping myself by any works of righteousness which I could do, I was brought, as I believed, to throw down my weapons and submit to God. The beauty, excellency, and propriety of his character and government, produced a calm serenity of mind, to which I was before a stranger. The conversation and society of the serious, gave me more satisfaction in one hour, than all the vain amusements which I could call to mind from my cradle until that time.

"I met with many trials from the gay company with which I had always lived in harmony; but for the most part, was enabled to encounter them with less difficulty than I expected. Returning from school, I met with a gentleman who had been absent during the time of my serious impressions. He accosted me in the following manner. 'How do you do, Miss ———? I hear you are serious, and have done dancing. Is it so?' I replied, 'that I had indeed refused to attend balls, for I believed I had already spent too much time in that folly; but feared I was not so serious as had been represented.' 'Well,' returned the gentleman, 'you have got a fit; but I am not much concerned; it will soon be over. I never knew an instance, but that in a short time those serious persons would be as gay as ever. I shall then remind you of what I now say; but you will tell me, I don't feel now as I did then.' He left me, for I was unable to answer. As soon as his face was turned, the tears flowed without control. I exclaimed to myself, '*O, is it possible? is it possible?* Can it be that I shall be left to that miserable resort for happiness?' I tried to believe that he prophesied falsely; but still I knew that it was not impossible. For sometime, I was much distressed lest I should be left to dishonor the cause of religion, and bring contempt upon its professors. About the age of nineteen, this over-anxious concern, as I then thought it, left my mind by degrees, and I lost much of the sense of my dependence. I heard too much of the applause of my fellow worms, which gave a spring to pride and self-conceit, till, alas! they gained an unhappy ascendency. I was now frequently in company with those who were indeed *civil*, but not *serious*, and joined in their trifling amusements. Their attention and politeness concealed the danger, and led me to be more and more conversant with such scenes of folly. At the time of your ordination, when I was about twenty, I was solicited by a near relative, out of respect to some respectable acquaintance then present, to attend a ball. I knew he would not advise me to do any thing which he *judged* at all inconsistent with my profession. After considerable conversation, and with much reluctance, I consented to go; and I assure you, sir, there was not a person in the company who did not see me. After the interesting services of the day, and the solemn consecration of a minister to feed my soul with the bread of life, and the water of life, here I was in the ball-room, amid the thoughtless and the gay. Nor was this the last time. I was again where there was music and dancing. My Christian friends were alarmed, and reproved me; but with little effect. I had listened to the voice of flattery, and God had left me to reap the reward of my folly. I had almost lost sight of God, and was gliding down the stream of spiritual declension. But in mercy, God was pleased to stop me, to open my eyes, and to bring me to consideration. O, the distress, anxiety, fears and doubts which now harrowed up my soul. Darkness without, and darkness within! I sincerely thought that if I could have recalled the last twelve months, and have removed into some distant land, where I could never behold a face which I ever saw before, I should have chosen it, rather than to have brought the disgrace which I then felt that I had brought upon the church of Christ. My distress was unknown to any but myself, and nothing short of experience can conceive it. All my former feelings, with the gentleman's prediction, were brought fresh to mind, and every reflection tended to aggravate my crime and enhance my distress. A compassionate Saviour at length brought me to feel and say,

> ' His strokes were fewer than my crimes,
> And lighter than my guilt.'

"I think, sir, I can say from experience, that the amusements of the thoughtless are exceedingly detrimental to the Christian's growth in grace, calculated to keep the soul in leanness, and to render a person unhappy in a religious profession, and discontented with the world. Conscience is continually smiting and reproving, and as the Christian has more light than an infidel, he is, of course, more unhappy in the neglect of duty. To undertake to serve God and mammon, is a sure way to render life miserable; for both Scripture and experience tell us we cannot do it.

"If you judge that what I have written will be of use as a warning to my young brethren and sisters in Christ, you may dispose of it for that purpose."

The following cases will exhibit a general view of the exercises of those who have been subjects of the work. I give the account nearly in their own words, that they may speak for themselves, and testify what God has done for their souls.

A man aged fifty-five, gave me the following account. "I had little or no religious instruction till about the age of twenty-one; and except a few seasons of conviction, which were soon gone, my youth, and indeed my life, has been spent in stupidity. I was persuaded that I must, and that I could do something of myself, but continually put it off for a more convenient season, and lived without hope and without God in the world. I was much opposed to the doctrine of grace, and I wanted to ask ministers and others, whether they were really Christians according to their scheme of justification by faith alone. I offered my children in baptism because it was fashionable, and supposed I had so far done my duty. After some thought upon the doctrines of religion, I concluded that if the doctrine of election was true, I was not to blame.

Here I settled down at ease, and was in this situation when the religious attention began. I had a curiosity to hear and see, but felt no uncommon concern until I heard a sermon from these words, 'Come unto me all ye that labor and are heavy laden, and I will give you rest.' The word was set home with power, and my sins appeared as a thick cloud. I determined to submit myself to God, and thought I did; yet I felt unaccountably distressed. I thought I had done enough, but found no relief from the agony of my mind. My sinfulness appeared greater than I could before have believed. It lay upon me as an insupportable burden, until the anguish of my mind impelled me to cry out for mercy. One day being alone in the fields, I could not restrain my feelings, but for some time on my bended knees, cried aloud, 'Lord, have mercy on me! Lord, have mercy on me!' I had hitherto neglected family prayer; but now I resolved to begin the next Sabbath morning. The time came, but I could not pray. My distress was soon increased by reflection on this text, 'No man having put his hand to the plough, and looking back, is fit for the kingdom of heaven.' The word came with power; and I said, 'wo is me, for I don't pray in my family.' In the evening I attempted. I had many trials—some of them, perhaps, uncommon, and not profitable to relate. Still I was determined to be saved by the law. My heart rose against Gospel doctrines, especially the doctrine of election, which I hated. Yet I could find no rest in the law. That I had broken the law was manifest. This scripture was directly against me,—'Cursed is every one that continueth not in all things written in the book of the law to do them.' I could scarcely eat, drink, or sleep. I concluded there was no mercy for me, and that I was approaching the gates of despair. All this time, I was seeking salvation by works of the law. One morning I felt better, and enjoyed a serenity of mind for which I could not account. I was soon engaged in contemplation on this text,— 'For whosoever will save his life, shall lose it; and whosoever will lose his life for my sake, shall find it.' My mind immediately explained it thus: whosoever will save his life by resting on his own works of law, shall lose it; but whosoever will renounce all dependence on himself, and trust alone to grace in Christ, shall find it. In a moment, the fabric which I had so long and so obstinately endeavored to rear, tumbled to pieces. I wondered at the ignorance and folly of all my former attempts, and that I should mistake essentially in so plain a case.

The difficulty was soon removed by this text,— 'The natural man receiveth not the things of the Spirit of God, for they are foolishness unto him; neither can he know them, because they are spiritually discerned.' My mind dwelt upon these and other passages as upon a rich treasure newly found. I seemed really to come from darkness to light. The words I had often read; but there now appeared in them a heavenly beauty which I had never known before. I felt a desire to glorify God, who had contrived such an excellent scheme of salvation, and revealed it so plainly to man. I found that the Bible had been to me a sealed book, and that with all my gettings, I had never got a true understanding of the way of salvation by Jesus Christ. The whole scheme of gospel doctrines, especially election and divine sovereignty, which before made my heart rise up in enmity against God, now appeared glorious and lovely doctrines. I saw that all which I had done to obtain salvation was wholly selfish; that I was totally depraved, and that unless the doctrine of election was true, there could be no hope in my case. I perceived that all my opposition to the doctrines of grace originated in pride, because I was not willing that God should work in me to will and to do of his good pleasure. I now rejoiced that he did do it, and yet I found myself in the unimpaired possession of moral freedom. I thought before that I was right, and that God was wrong; but now I felt that God was right, and that I was wrong; and that my former scheme of salvation by works of the law, if it could be true, was not desirable, because unspeakably less beautiful than that by sovereign grace in Jesus Christ. I felt no desire to hear preaching about works, unless a clear distinction was made between duty and merit. I thought little of myself, or of the danger of future punishment. God was all-glorious and the Saviour the chiefest among ten thousand for his own sake. Having obtained help of God, I continue unto this time, a brand plucked out the fire. In myself, I am a poor, miserable, guilty creature; and if I am ever saved, it will manifestly be all of God. 'Not unto me, but unto God, through Christ, be all the glory forever.'"

A young woman addressed me by letter as follows: "My design in this communication, is to inform you what the Lord hath done for my soul. At the time of my first serious impressions, I was sixteen years old, and had, to that time, lived a careless, stupid life; a stranger to God and Christ, and to things sacred and divine.

I thought I was not very bad, as I refrained from stealing, lying, swearing, and other open violations of God's law; not considering that he looks at the heart. I thought I was too young to attend much to religion, and I considered it a sad and melancholy thing, fit for none but those who were just about to leave the world. I depended much on the doctrine of election, as I had perverted it. If I am to be saved, I shall be saved, let me do what I will; and if I am to be lost, I shall be lost, let me do what I will. Here I rested, secure in my sinful neglect of God and his Son Jesus Christ. And I fear that many who are older and wiser than I, rest on the same sandy foundation. I had a great taste for reading, but I read those books only which served to poison my mind, and lead it from God and serious things. When the awakening appeared among us, and one and another of my companions were inquiring what they should do to be saved? I resolved to go on as I was, let the consequences be what they would. I lived from home, and hearing that my aged parents and two of my sisters were under great concern of mind, I could not forbear sighing and saying to myself, are they all fools? I shall never enjoy another moment's comfort with them as long as

I live. It appeared to me that I would not feel as they for the whole world.

"The first serious impression on my mind, was while reading these lines in the 'Young Child's Pious Resolutions,'—

> ' 'Tis time to seek to God, and pray
> For what I want for every day;
> I have a precious soul to save,
> And I a mortal body have.'

I had hitherto thought that there would be time enough for me to attend to religion when I was *old;* but these words came with such power that I could not rest without seeking an interest in Christ *immediately.* I was greatly concerned about myself, and felt that I must do something; but what to do, I knew not. I could not pray, and never had prayed in my whole life. I dared not repeat the Lord's prayer, because I thought it was made for his disciples, and not for me. I resolved that no one should know my feelings, but soon my distress poured in upon me like a flood, and I could not forbear crying to the Saviour for mercy. I attended meeting the next Sabbath, expecting to find some relief, when these awful words were the subject of discourse, 'It shall be more tolerable for the land of Sodom in the day of judgment than for thee.' My sins rose in order before me. I was struck dumb before God while these words sounded in my ears, and the sermon described my awful case. Instead of finding comfort, I went home with a heavy heart. I soon began to doubt whether the Bible was the word of God. I thought it might possibly be a forgery, and earnestly hoped it was. I hated the Bible, because it contained my condemnation. I felt that God was partial in showing mercy to others and not to me. The enmity of my heart rose against him; and indeed, I wished there was no God. I attempted to cast the blame upon him, and justify myself; but still could not be satisfied. I longed to be spoken out of existence, for the more I understood of the divine character, the more I hated it; and I could not endure the thought that the Lord reigned, and that all things were at his disposal. When I heard of some who had obtained comfort, and had not been so long in distress as I had, my heart boiled within me. I thought I could not live long in this distress, and that God would not suffer such a wicked wretch to live; and even death appeared desirable, though it should make me eternally miserable; because while living, I thought I was preparing for a more aggravated punishment. While walking, I sometimes imagined that the earth would open and swallow me up; and that I hung over the bottomless pit by nothing but the brittle thread of life. I slept but little, for if I went to sleep, I was afraid I should awake in hell. In this unhappy state of mind I continued from September, 1799, to March, 1800, when I was taken dangerously sick, and for some days deprived of reason. When my reason returned, I supposed I must soon die; but how different were my feelings now from what they had formerly been! God appeared to me perfectly just and righteous in all his dealings with me. It appeared to be right and reasonable that I should love such a holy being. I felt more composed and tranquil than ever before; and I could say with the man restored to sight, 'whereas I was blind, now I see.' I saw such a beauty and loveliness in God, and the things which I before hated, that I seemed to be in a new world, where every thing spoke the glory of God. He appeared to be so holy, righteous and good in all his works and dispensations, that I could freely submit myself to him, and say with Job, 'Though he slay me, yet will I trust in him.' When I recovered so as to wait on God in his house, I enjoyed more delight in one day, than in all the balls and vain amusements which I had attended in my life. God and his services have ever since appeared glorious to me, and O that

I may glorify him in life, death, and eternity. My hope depends solely on the rich, free, and sovereign grace of God in Jesus Christ."

A young married woman gives the following account:

"Near the close of September, 1799, while I enjoyed a comfortable state of health, a religious meeting was attended at our house. I found myself somewhat impressed with a sense of sin, and thought that I wished to be a Christian. A day or two after this meeting my health rapidly declined. I was soon dangerously ill, and to appearance, on the borders of the grave. My great concern was to recover my health, and my hope rested on the physician, and not on Christ. My situation grew more and more alarming, and my friends viewed me as near the end of life. I was in some measure alarmed, and much feared that if I should die, I should be eternally miserable. I endeavored to satisfy myself by reflecting that I was not so guilty as others. Except when people were talking to me of faith, repentance and the new-birth, I always doubted whether the justice of a holy God would send me to hell for the few crimes which I had committed. Alas, how little did I know of the evil nature of sin, and of my own criminality before God! And all this while I was viewed by others as on the borders of eternity. Indeed, sir, your conversation, at the time of your visits, and the conversation of other religious people, was never sufficient to drive me wholly from this refuge. Neither your prayers, nor the apparent near approach of death, ever excited in my mind any degree of anxious concern for my soul. The idea of leaving my husband and children, appeared the most distressing. But I chose not to hear the subject mentioned, and endeavored to keep it from my mind as much as possible. A beneficent God at length interposed in my behalf, rebuked my painful disorder, and restored me to my family as one ransomed from the grave. But I was as stupid under the mercies of God, as I had been before under his chastening hand. Nothing could make my heart submit. I was stupid when brought to the brink of the grave, with an eternity of wo before me; and I was stupid when marvelously restored to health. The world, with all its delusive charms, now presented itself to my view. As soon as I was able to ride out, I visited an elder brother, who conversed with me freely on my situation, and the mercies which I had received. I observed to him that I really wished to become religious, but I was certain that it was not in my power. He replied, that it was impossible for him to tell for what purpose my life had been so remarkably preserved; but that from my apparent stupidity, there was great reason to fear that it was, that I might have an opportunity of filling up the measure of my iniquities. The idea struck me, and seemed the voice of warning from God to me to answer for my ingratitude. The sins of my past life rose, and were set in order before me. I soon found that I had abused all the mercies of God, that there was a holy law which I had transgressed, and that I was under its just, though awful curse. I rested but little the following night, and my distress continued for several days. I was again about to go back; but the following Sabbath I attended meeting, when a thank-offering was presented for my recovery. Here my conviction and distress revived, and continued through the week. The next Sabbath I heard a sermon from these words, 'Ephraim is joined to his idols, let him alone.' The sermon was applicable, as I thought, to my case, and seemed to be addressed to me in particular. My convictions increased, until I found myself hanging over the pit of everlasting wo, destitute of the least merit, and wounded by reflection on a whole life spent in rebellion against God. Although I was convinced that I had hitherto been kept in existence by the forbearance of God, yet now it appeared to me that I so richly deserved his wrath and curse, that I had nothing else to expect. With these views I again attended meeting, and found the same broken law flaming against me, and bringing my iniquity before my face. I returned home, took my Bible and retired; and while perusing the sacred pages, this thought arose in my mind, 'Jesus has died for sinners.' It filled my heart with joy, and although in my agony of mind, I had not very clear views of Christ as Mediator, yet the idea was now sweet and refreshing to my weary and heavy laden soul. After a few weeks, I found myself, as I believed, willing to come to the feet of Jesus, and lie low in the dust before him. My comfort was all built on Christ as the foundation; and I think he then appeared, and still appears lovely as he is in himself, and will be so forever, whatever becomes of me. During my convictions, I had many heart-risings against God and the doctrines of grace; but when this enmity was slain by the Holy Spirit, in a way which I know not, God appeared just and righteous; Christ the chiefest among ten thousand, and altogether lovely; and the doctrines of grace the sweet food of my soul, the manna from heaven. Indeed, sir, I have been such an ungrateful, blind, and stupid sinner, that I am sure there can be no hope in my case, unless there is a remnant according to the election of grace. My attainments are so far short of what I should suppose would be in a real Christian, that I am especially at times, doubtful whether I shall ever obtain a seat at the right hand of Christ. But if this should ever be, I shall be less than the least of all saints, and must forever disclaim any merit in myself; lay my crown at the feet of Immanuel, and ascribe all to his meritorious righteousness. Let the praise and the glory be forever to his electing love, to rich, free and sovereign grace."

CHAPTER XVIII.

An account of a Revival of Religion in Brookfield, Vt., in the year 1801. By the Rev. Elijah Lyman.

For a number of years after my settlement in the work of the gospel ministry in this place, there was a great degree of indifference and stupidity, respecting those things which accompany salvation, both in the minds of professors and others. In this time of declension among us, and the adjacent towns, errors of various kinds increased, especially those of the Arians, Socinians, Arminians, and Universalists. Our articles of faith were expressed in very short and general terms, to which those embracing the above mentioned errors, as they said, could consistently subscribe. It was thought, therefore, expedient to revise them, that we might be the better guarded against heresy in the church.

In the year 1800 it was proposed to the church, whether it would not be advisable to revise their articles of faith, and make them more explicit and intelligible; not faulting the old confession for what it did express, but for what it did not.

The proposition met with a favorable reception in the minds of the brethren present; and they requested me to bring forward such a revision as I should think proper.

According to the desire of the church, I soon presented them with such articles of Christian faith as I conceived to be agreeable to the tenor of the holy Scriptures, in which I endeavored to bring clearly into view the leading and fundamental doctrines of the gospel; such as original sin; the total depravity of the human heart; the sovereignty of God; the divinity of Jesus

Christ, and God's electing love through him; the necessity and efficacy of divine grace in the regeneration, sanctification, and perseverance of the saints; the inexcusableness and criminality of impenitence; and the endless punishment of the wicked in the coming world.

When these articles were laid before the church for their consideration and remarks, it appeared that they were not fully understood, or were absolutely opposed by some of the members. It was therefore proposed by some of the brethren, and unanimously voted, to request me to illustrate and vindicate those articles which I had presented to the church, in public sermons on the Sabbath. I felt it my duty to comply with so reasonable a request; desiring at the same time that they would hear me patiently, till a fair opportunity was given, fully to discuss those important and fundamental principles of the Christian religion.

Having this request granted, I entered upon the arduous undertaking, which I conceived would be the more difficult, as I was satisfied that there were those among us who were fixedly opposed to some of the leading articles contained in the confession. While I continued in my public discourses on the Sabbath, to illustrate the truths expressed in the articles proposed to be adopted by the church, it proved the occasion of great controversy and contention, and was the common subject of debate among the people of almost every class, both on the Lord's day while out of public worship, and through the week. The contention was so great, that it was truly alarming in the view of some, who professed to be friendly both to me and to the doctrines which were delivered. They thought it advisable, for the present, to desist from preaching them. But as they were considered to be the truths of God, and the great pillars of the gospel, in which the divine honor was peculiarly concerned, and without the vindication of which, we, as God's dependent creatures, could not expect his divine interposition and grace in the conviction and salvation of sinners, I was decided in my opinion, that it was my indispensable duty to proceed, till I should have gone through the whole system, according to the request of the church.

Agreeably to this resolution, I continued to illustrate, in regular order, those truths expressed in the revised articles of faith, every Lord's day, for more than a year, only when some special occasion required a different subject. But before I had accomplished this laborious undertaking, I found, to my unspeakable joy and satisfaction, that indeed the Lord was on our side, by his special grace, applying to the hearts and consciences of the people those gospel truths which I had been laboring to illustrate and enforce, and which some had been equally opposing.

The first appearance of the work was upon a man of about forty-five years of age, who was not more friendly to the cause of truth than all natural men; yet he did not attend to, or regard the subject of religion enough to oppose it. His heart and mind were wholly swallowed up in the pursuit of worldly wealth. It might be said of him that "the cares of the world, and the deceitfulness of riches choked the Word, that it became unfruitful." By his own account it appeared, that he had been under serious impressions for about two years, although this was not known by any person, even the wife of his bosom, until after he thought he was made a subject of divine grace.

This was very unexpected, and therefore very surprising to the people. It was on Lord's day, March 15th, 1801. As the temper of his heart was apparently renewed, so his conversation was on new subjects, even spiritual and divine things, which from his mouth had never been heard before.

It is hardly conceivable with what astonishment his friends and neighbors would stand and admire the gracious words which dropped from his lips, while he spoke to them of the infinite value of their souls, and the importance of being interested in that happiness which Christ had purchased for poor, perishing sinners. He, from experience, admonished them of having their souls ensnared with worldly subjects, to the great neglect of that good part which cannot be taken away. This called up the attention of some, particularly to the subject of experimental religion, and led them to conceive it to be a reality.

About a month after this there was another very unexpected conversion. An old gentleman who had entered upon the seventy-sixth year of his age, and had spent his days, to that advanced period, in sin. He was particularly noted for profaneness and irreligion. Being rationally convinced that he was in the last part of his life, he began to think it necessary to have some religion when he died, or he must be wretched. For about three years previous to his conversion, he embraced the scheme of universal salvation. He had been taught that Christ died to effect the salvation of all men, that his work was done, that his happiness was secure, and that he had nothing to fear—that if he would believe the doctrine, he might take the comfort of it and die in peace. Such preaching as this being perfectly agreeable to a heart long accustomed to the love and practice of sin, he most cordially embraced and rested thereon, as the only foundation of his hope, in which he expected to live and die. But at this time, one stronger than the strong man armed, came upon him and overcame him, and took from him all his armor wherein he trusted, and divided his spoils. When he brought eternal things into view, his hope fled like chaff before the wind. He found himself in a lost and wretched condition, without God, and without hope in the world, and eternity just before him.

But it pleased God, of his abundant mercy, to appear for him, in this critical moment, and pluck him as a brand from the burning, and give his soul to rejoice at the manifestation of God's glorious character, as a righteous and just God, who would eternally vindicate his own law and character against wicked men and devils. This proved to a demonstration to observing minds, among his acquaintance, that a man when he was old both in years and sin, could be born again. His following life and conversation bespake that he was created anew in Christ Jesus, and that his great aim was to live to the glory of God. To use his own words, being asked how old he was, about eighteen or twenty months after his conversion, he replied, " Through divine goodness, I have had an existence in God's world seventy-seven years; but I have not lived two."

This very singular instance was the means of impressing the minds of those who were within the circle of his particular acquaintance.

There was an unusual collection on the Sabbath, and attention to the Word preached, with an increased application for public lectures, in different quarters of the town, through the course of the week.

About this time it pleased the great Dispenser of divine grace to call two others out of the kingdom of darkness into his marvelous light.

One was a woman, who, in the view of her most intimate acquaintance, was thought to be a Christian, and at certain times she was ready to conclude the same of herself, which opinion was grounded upon her external morality. But now she was brought to realize that her former hope would be as the spider's web and the giving up of the ghost. She found by diligent self-examination, as she expressed herself, that she had lived forty years in the world, and had never given her heart to the Lord.

At a public conference held at the meeting-house, where was a large assembly collected, after that woman had obtained a wonderful relief in her mind, at the desire of a number of Christian friends, she related before them all, the great trials through which she had passed, and the mistaken opinion which she, and perhaps others might have entertained respecting her Christian character; and also the way and manner in which God had been manifested to her soul. She expressed her strong attachment to, and delight in the Saviour of lost men, as being superior to every worldly object and human character. She most urgently invited all who were strangers to Christ and the excellency of the gospel salvation, to come, taste, and see that the Lord is good. Those who might have had a hope that they were Christians, she exhorted to give all diligence, and see that their hearts were right with God. All which was done in such an interesting, pathetic and feeling manner, that there was scarcely a tearless eye in the whole assembly. This being accompanied by the power of divine grace, proved an occasion of giving the work a more general and thorough spread through the different parts of the town, both among professors and non-professors. This was truly a very searching time. Many awoke from their sleepy profession, and shaking themselves as from the dust, expressed a new zeal and engagedness for the prosperity of Zion. Others were shaken even from their foundation, being constrained to give up their former hopes, as refuges of deception and lies, and were led to begin their work anew, laying the foundation of their hope alone upon Christ their rock. And others, who had expressed the greatest indifference, both in respect to their own, and the salvation of others, now were brought with attention and anxiety to inquire, "What shall we do to be saved?"

For several months, it was a very serious time among us. The mind of almost every one was struck with an unusual solemnity. The attention of many was called up to the momentous concerns of eternity. We have reason to fear, however, but few were chosen subjects of regenerating grace. The number of thirty have been added to the church, in this revival. Others retain their serious impressions, and still give evidence that they are friendly to Christ and his cause, yet neglect publicly to profess his name, through self-diffidence, and a jealousy over the deceitfulness of their own hearts, lest they should proclaim that to the world, which they had never done heartily to the Lord. I cannot, however, but hope that ere long the darkness will be dispelled, and their doubts removed, which at present seem to obstruct thei way, in coming forward publicly to profess Christ before this adulterous generation.

This work of the Holy Spirit seemed to affect, principally, the minds of parents and heads of families, although the attention of youth was arrested for a time, to consider what these things meant. There were but one or two instances of hopeful conversion among the youth. This I suppose to be different from what is true of revivals in general.

Among those whose minds were the most seriously impressed, it was a common observation, the present call from God to them by his Holy Spirit, was, most probably, the last they should ever receive, and should they resist and grieve away the heavenly messenger, they should never expect again to have their attention called to spiritual concerns, but be left to hardness of heart, and blindness of mind, till they were ripe for endless ruin. Thus, in their own view, they could say as it respected themselves, "Behold now is the accepted time; behold now is the day of salvation." Nothing was more terrifying to them, than the thought of returning back to their former state of thoughtless security. The trials of many while under convictions, were peculiarly great and pressing. I recollect the observation of one while under the pressure of her own guilt, and the threatening of the divine law. She said, "I could cheerfully be burnt at the stake, if thereby I might be liberated from my present distress for my soul. Nothing but the precious blood of Christ can cleanse the soul from sin, and liberate us from the condemning sentence of that law, which is holy, just, and good."

Some persons, at first, seemed to discover great beauty in the divine character, and to be greatly transported with joy and delight, but in process of time were ready to give up their hope, from a view of the great wickedness of their hearts. Many were ready to say, "Can it be that a heart so vile as mine, was ever renewed by the Holy Ghost?" From this consideration there was a great backwardness in the minds of many, in coming forward to join themselves to the visible church of Christ, lest by their irregular conduct they should wound the cause of their dear Lord, and coming unworthily to the Lord's table, they should eat and drink judgment to themselves.

The work, so far as we are able to discern, has been genuine. Not a single instance of apostacy has appeared among those who have given us charitable ground to hope they were the subjects of regenerating grace.

Those doctrines of divine grace, which met with such violent opposition among the people previous to the awakening, were now witnessed and confirmed by the experience and declaration of those who were hopefully enlightened and sanctified by the Spirit of Truth. When the Lord opened their hearts, they no longer disputed their total vileness, and the necessity of the powerful and energetic influences of the Holy Spirit to create them anew; and that it was of the Lord to have mercy on whom he would have mercy. The doctrine of election, in particular, which some could not contemplate but with abhorrence, and which they were wont to esteem very discouraging to sinners, now became their only encouragement and hope, and was sweeter to them than honey or the honey-comb.

This, however, is not the case with all. The beauty of those doctrines, to some, appears to be hid, as was said by an inspired apostle: "If our gospel be hid, it is hid to them that are lost, in whom the God of this world hath blinded the minds of them that believe not, lest the light of the glorious gospel of Christ, who is the image of God, should shine unto them."

But if it may be agreeable to the purpose of God, it is our earnest prayer, and constant labor that they might be savingly acquainted with God and themselves, and the truth as it is in Jesus Christ.

From my own experience and observation, I am fully persuaded that my labor, the year preceding the revival, in illustrating and enforcing the important and fundamental doctrines of the gospel, which, in their own nature, tend to exalt God, and abase the feelings of corrupt men, was as great a means in the hand of God, of producing that spiritual harvest which we received the year following, as richly manuring and faithfully cultivating the natural soil, is a direct means of producing a plentiful harvest in the field. It was like breaking up the fallow ground, and did so convince the understandings of carnal and selfish minds, that when the gentle dews of divine grace descended, they were prepared for the reception of the good seed of the Word; and it sprang up and bare fruit thirty fold, to the praise of God's efficacious grace.

CHAPTER XIX.

An account of a Revival of Religion in KILLINGWORTH, CONN., in the years 1801, 1802 and 1803. By the Rev. JOSIAH B. ANDREWS.

In the latter part of the month of April, 1801, a number of the young people requested that a sermon might be preached to them, upon election day, which they had formerly observed as a day of feasting and merriment. The proposal, at first, was made to me by two or three only, and I declined it, thinking it inexpedient upon that day, when there seemed to be no special reason for it. As yet I had no knowledge of any special seriousness beginning in the place, neither was any thing of the kind suggested by them. But the solicitation being renewed, and by a large number, I consented to preach, though upon a different day. Still ignorant of their design, I endeavored to adapt the sermon to their age and condition in life, hoping it might be useful. There was a full assembly of old as well as young, and solemn attention. At this time the Spirit of the Lord was secretly working in them, though there was nothing further said, until the evening of the 10th of

May following, when about fifty persons desired a conference, that evening, or a discourse upon the subject of religion. On seeing such a number collected, inquiring for the crucified Jesus, I was so struck with the solemn appearance, that, for a few moments, I was at a loss what was wisest to be done. After serious reflection, hoping God would give me assistance, I concluded to address them on these words—"Now, therefore, are we all here present before God, to hear all things that are commanded thee of God." They seemed to be much moved by the subject.

Perceiving that the Spirit of the Lord was, in very deed, in this place, and in a peculiar manner shedding his benign influence on the sinful children of men, it was deemed expedient to appoint weekly conferences for the encouragement of such a work, which began in the manner above mentioned, and they have been constantly and punctually attended until this time.

The conferences, at first, were looked upon by some in an unfavorable point of light, and supposed to be party meetings, instituted to divide the society still more and more; and those who were known to be under convictions of sin, were supposed to be falling into a kind of delirium. Notwithstanding, the work was gradually carried on till there was a fuller display of God's sovereignty and grace, upon the 9th and 10th of August, at which time I was about to leave the society, for several months at least, if not finally, to fulfill a previous engagement. It appeared expedient, therefore, to invite those who were under serious impressions to meet at my lodgings for religious conversation. Accordingly upon the Sabbath I informed the congregation that there would be such a meeting, at two o'clock the next day. In the evening about forty came in for religious instruction, and on the next day the house was filled, generally through the day, especially in the afternoon. More than two hundred were present, anxious about their salvation, till sometime in the evening, when they reluctantly retired. At this time about sixty were found deeply affected with a sense of the plague of their own hearts, and the others seriously alarmed, according to the words of the prophet, "Sinners in Zion are afraid; fearfulness hath surprised the hypocrite."

Several having passed the night in sorrow, came again very early in the morning, much affected at the recollection of their past offences, crying, "Men and brethren, what shall we do?" Under these affecting circumstances, I was called to leave this distressed people. They were much affected at the thought of being left without a preached gospel, as it seemed they must be, at such a time as this. They had nowhere to go but unto God, to whom they ought to have repaired before; but depending too much on human aid, they were at last left to feel their absolute dependence on the Great Proprietor of all, and nothing remained for them to do but to repent and believe. Under their distress of soul, they cried for mercy, and shortly after numbers rejoiced in hope.

In the months of September, October, November, and December, thirty-two hopeful converts were added to the church. After this, I returned and ministered to the people again, and on the 21st of April following, I took the pastoral charge of this church. This year, which was 1802, seventeen only were visibly brought into Christ's kingdom by a profession of Christianity. The year following, 1803, the attention of both old and young seemed to be unusually excited again, and thirty-three were added to our communion. Since the beginning of the present year, nine have been admitted, making in the whole, ninety-one; forty-six males and forty-five females. They are of different ages, from seventy down to eighteen, though the greatest part are in youth and middle life. A number more entertain comfortable hopes, and it is expected that they will soon publicly profess their faith in Christ.

A few instances it may not be improper to notice.

A person about twenty-three years of age, and now a respectable member of the church, communicated the following account.

"Through childhood and youth, I was equal to, if not surpassing any of my companions in lightness and vanity. Though free from profaneness and the grossest sins, I thought little of God, or of a future state, until I was about nineteen years old, except at two periods which I perfectly remember—at one of which I was so impressed, for a few hours, with the thoughts of eternity, that I earnestly wished for death. All this was soon forgotten, and I went on uninterruptedly in my folly again, until I was about fifteen, when my attention was again excited by the things of religion. I now felt it my duty to pray, and made the attempt with the determination to continue it, which I did, but very carelessly, and soon after very thoughtlessly, once or twice a week. This formal service blunted the stings of my conscience, so that I passed quietly along, trusting in the advantages of living in a Christian land, and of a religious education to save me; until it pleased God, in his own time and way, to convince me that a change of heart is necessary to an entrance into heaven. About the middle of the summer of 1800, I began to entertain hard and blasphemous thoughts of God, which I endeavored to suppress, but in vain. The more I strove against them, the greater ascendency they gained over me, and notwithstanding the strongest opposition which I could make to them, they filled me with horror.

"Having tried all human ways, in vain, to obtain relief from my horrors of mind, no help seemed to remain, but that which is in Christ; and when I thought to go unto him, as the last resort, I was so fully persuaded that I should be rejected for my blasphemous thoughts, that I chose rather to continue in my suffering state, feeling myself exposed to all the wrath of an offended God, and bearing the pain of a guilty conscience, for more than six months incessantly. At the end of this period, as I was one day thinking over my deplorable condition, the idea that I might yet be saved, suddenly came into my mind, and that Christ died for sinners, even the greatest, and that his grace was sufficient for me; but a review of my past conduct, and my feelings, as they were then, showed me the absurdity of looking for salvation from one of whom I had entertained such a wrong opinion. This gave an additional weight to my heavy burden, which increased upon me from July till April, when I heard a sermon from these words—' Whosoever shall speak a word against the Son of Man, it shall be forgiven him, but unto him that blasphemeth against the Holy Ghost, it shall not be forgiven.' This sermon had a singular effect upon me. The words, when first read, moved me to keen despair, and for a short time, the pains of hell got hold upon me; but before the discourse was finished, I ventured to hope that I had not committed the sin unto death. But alas! little did I think of the conflict yet to be endured, which was dreadful above all I had experienced before. Doubts as to the existence of a God began to fill my mind. To ease my mind, I determined to dwell no longer on so gloomy a subject; but a pained conscience would not suffer me to rest, and the fear of atheism aggravatedly oppressed me, till it pleased the Most High, in a sovereign manner, graciously to enable me, as I hope, to stay my soul on Jesus Christ. With earnest desires I sought him, and with patience I followed on to know him, having resolved that if I perished, it should be at his feet. In kindness he seemed to manifest himself unto me, and to say, Come hither, I am the way, leave the tempter and thy sins, trust in me, and I will love thee. Thanks be to God, from that time I have been enabled to say, 'Though he slay me, yet will I trust in him.'

"For nearly three years past my mind has been, generally, comfortable, though I have not been altogether without fear that I might be deceived by the treachery of my depraved heart. Therefore I have, at several periods, by reason of a jealousy over myself, sought to revive former painful convictions of mind, but the power to do so is gone, and I cannot recall it.

"A kind of sweet, tranquil joy, to which I was a stranger before, now fills my soul whenever I contemplate the works of God, and call to mind his holy character, especially when I read his Word, and lift up my heart in prayer. The greatness of that joy which I first received after a year's wandering in darkness, and almost inconceivable distress, after a short time passed away, and I have now no other than that described above, except that it increases, and at times rises to a greater degree, flowing out towards all mankind, desiring their salvation in conformity to the will of God. One cause of my being so long distressed with a conviction of sin, was, doubtless, my sinful bashfulness, which kept me from communicating my thoughts to any one, even to my most intimate friends. The tempter, by means of this, had an advantage over me, and caused me to counterfeit a cheerful behavior when my soul was filled with great distress. If I had taken counsel in my awakenings, it now appears as if I should have been saved the most of my anguish; but if Christ may be glorified thereby, I desire to be still, and to know that he is God."

Another instance which I would mention, is a youth who speaks thus:

"Knowing by experience the deplorable state of a sinner, that he is by nature totally destitute of love and conformity to God, and that he cannot be saved but by a special act of sovereign grace, induceth me to ask for further instruction upon this all-important subject, and to communicate in a summary manner the state of my mind, and the feelings with which it has been exercised.

"From my earliest age, I endeavored to lead a moral life, being often taught that God would punish sinners; but I did not believe that I should suffer for the few offences of which I had been guilty. Having avoided many sins which

I saw in others, I imagined all was well with me, till I was about eighteen years old, when I heard a sermon preached upon the necessity of regeneration, which put me upon thinking of the need of a change of heart in myself. I did not, however, well receive the discourse at the time; for I was sensible that I knew nothing about such a change, neither did I wish to know, for I believed myself to be as good as others, without it; and to be equal with them, I thought would be sufficient. However, the thought troubled me considerably, from day to day, and caused me to think of praying, which I had never done, except repeating some form as a little child, and doing it to remove the stings of a guilty conscience, when I considered myself in imminent danger. Sometime after this I heard another sermon, which convinced me that I had quenched the Spirit, which occasioned the most alarming fears that I should be left to eat of the fruit of my own ways. Supposing that I was alone in the thoughts of eternity, I separated myself from all company, and determined to seek an interest in Christ. I concluded that something must be done to appease God's anger. I read, and prayed, and strove in every possible way to prepare myself to go to God, that I might be saved from his wrath. The more I strove in this selfish way, the more anxious I was, and no help was given. Soon I began to murmur and repine, and I accused God of the greatest injustice in requiring me to turn to him, and while I was striving with all my might, as I thought, he appeared not to regard me. I considered God as obligated to save me, because I had done so much for him, and finding no relief, I wished he might not be, and began really to doubt the truth of his holy Word, and to disbelieve his existence, for if there were a God, I perfectly hated him. I searched the Scriptures daily, hoping to find inconsistencies in them, to condemn the Bible because it was against me; and while I was diligently pursuing my purpose, every thing which I read, and every sermon which I heard condemned me. Christian conversation gave me great distress. I tried to repent, but I could not feel the least sorrow for my innumerable sins. By endeavoring to repent, I saw that my heart still remained impenitent. Although I knew that I hated every thing serious, yet I determined to habituate myself to the duties which God required, to see if I could not by that means be made to love him; and I continued in this state some months. The fear of having committed the unpardonable sin, now began to arise in my mind, and I could find no rest day nor night. When my weary limbs demanded sleep, the fear of awaking in a miserable eternity prevented me from closing my eyes, and nothing gave me ease. No voice of mirth or sound whatever was heard, but what reminded me of the awful day when God shall bring every work into judgment. All self-righteousness failed me, and having no confidence in God, I was left in deep despondency. After a while, a surprising tremor seized all my limbs, and death appeared to have taken hold on me. Eternity, the word eternity, sounded louder than any human voice I ever heard, and every moment of time appeared infinitely more valuable than all the wealth of the world. Not long after this an unusual calmness pervaded my soul, which I thought little of at first, except that I was freed from my awful convictions, and this sometimes grieved me, as I feared I had lost all conviction. Soon after hearing the feelings of a Christian described, I took courage and thought I knew by experience what they were. The character of God and the doctrines of the Bible, which I could not meditate upon before without hatred, especially those of election and free grace, now appear delightful, and the only means by which, through grace, dead sinners can be made the living sons of God. My heart feels its sinfulness. To sorrow for it, affords that joy which my tongue cannot express. Were I sensible that at death my hope would perish, yet it seems to me now that I could not willingly quit the service of God, nor the company of Christians; but my unfaithfulness often makes me doubt my sincerity, and should I at last be raised to glory, all the praise will be to God for the exhibition of his sovereign grace."

Another person nearly forty years of age, at a private lecture attended April 22d, 1801, was so wrought upon by the Word being set home upon his heart, that he instantly became so overcome with a sense of his danger, that he was scarcely able to stand. He says—

"I looked round for something to stay myself with. Fearing lest some one should ask, what aileth thee? I endeavored to bear up under the pressure as much as possible, and so concealed the matter. This, however, put me upon inquiring what I should do to be saved, for previously I had little or no anxiety about my future state. Soon after this I set up family prayer, which I had never attempted before. In the beginning it was hard, but I felt it to be my duty, and was unable to rest in the neglect of it. Having many serious thoughts, and loving, as I imagined, the service of God, I went forward and made a public profession of religion, and believed all was well, until the 22d of November following, when upon the Lord's day it was observed in the sermon, that persons might be strict in all the outward forms and duties of religion, and still be in the gall of bitterness and bonds of iniquity; for without holiness no man shall see the Lord. We must be born again. It immediately occurred to me that I was one of that description.

"I had made a profession of religion, but I was conscious that I had never felt it. This lay with great weight on my mind. As I was walking a few evenings after this distress began, the first thing I recollect, after I left the house where I had been, I was standing still more than half a mile distant from the place I had left, reasoning with myself in this manner;—What, must man be born again? Is this a work of the Holy Spirit? Is God a Sovereign, having mercy on whom he will have mercy? Are not these doctrines in the Bible? Yes, I know they are, for I have often read them. Why then should we not hear them? For all that God has taught is good, and nothing to be refused. Surely we ought. O, what shall I do? I will not open my mouth against them. Thus I was weary and heavy laden, and continued until Thanksgiving day, when I began more sensibly to fear that I should be of all men the most miserable. In the evening I went again to one of my neighbors, in order to divert my mind; but in vain. The cheerly conversation of my neighbor increased my sorrow. I wondered how any one could laugh or smile. When I returned and attempted to commend my house in prayer to God, I was more distressed than ever, for I began to feel my spiritual blindness, especially in prayer, for my form was gone, and I could not recall it. I experienced the same again the next morning. When I took my Bible in my hands, I had such a tremor that I could not read, and could scarcely speak, so that I went out ashamed and confounded. I endeavored to pursue my secular business, but it was with great indifference, for my soul was full of anguish, till by sovereign grace it was brought home to God. About the middle of the day on the next Friday, I had such manifestations of God's love, and such admiring thoughts of his holy character, and of all the precepts of the gospel which my soul so much detested before, that I could no longer hold my peace. I immediately left all, repaired to my dwelling, and called upon my companion to help me praise the Lord. 'Praise the Lord, O sing praises to our God,' was the language of my soul through the day. Now I wanted all around me to taste the loving kindness of our God, and to bless his holy name. Since that time, I have had a variety of feelings, and hours of darkness, but I cannot give up my hope in Christ."

There are two other persons of different ages—one is in early life—who have been remarkably tempted and buffeted of Satan, as they fully believe. One of them seemed to be forced, as it were, to take life, so that for a number of days he feared to take a knife in his hand, or any other sharp tool, for it seemed as though it must necessarily be put to the throat, even without its being desired; but God in due time afforded relief, and afterwards filled that soul with peculiar joy.

The other was an instance of great temptation in secret prayer. While thus distressed with temptations, "It came into my mind," he says, "that I needed divine assistance. Immediately my whole heart and soul appeared to ascend to heaven with this fervent petition, that God would condescend to meet me in the closet and graciously assist me in conquering the tempter, that I might no more be led captive by him at his will. I do not remember all the words which I used, but I began my petition thus—'Holy, holy, holy, Lord God Almighty.' The answer which I received was not by an audible voice, but the fact that God had heard and would grant my request, was as evident as if it had been by a voice. This was a precious season, and I felt astonished at my stupidity that I had never before thought of looking to God for assistance. When it was morning, I took my Bible and retired to my closet, and began my devotions, asking God to meet with me—and such sensible and sweet communion with God I never thought of enjoying before. I proceeded renewedly to enter into covenant with my Maker, which, as it appears to me, I did with all my heart, dedicating myself to his service, both soul and body, for time and eternity. I could now truly say, 'Lord, it is good for me to be here. One hour spent in thy service is better than ten thousand spent elsewhere.'

"The night following, after resting awhile, I awoke and felt as if I was actually encircled in the arms of my dear Redeemer. No tongue can describe the bliss which I felt. I concluded it must be what Peter expresses in this manner—'Whom having not seen ye love, and in whom, though now ye see him not, yet believing, ye rejoice with joy unspeakable and full of glory.' These words also made a deep impression on my mind—'They that know thy name will put their trust in thee.'

"For eight or ten days, I had an hour or two each morning, before light, of enjoying the sweetest communion with my Saviour, that it is possible for finite creatures to enjoy, in this imperfect state. The Spirit did not leave me until it had, seemingly, led my mind to a comprehensive view of the character of God and of all his precepts. Lastly, I had a most realizing view of the odious nature of sin, and the wonderful patience of God in bearing so long with impenitent sinners. From that time, my greatest anxiety has been to cease from sin, and no temptation has overtaken me but such as is common to men."

The persons mentioned in this narrative have all of them been hopefully in the school of Christ more than three years, and some of them much longer; which must have been some trial of their faith, and affords a comfortable hope that the things which they have experienced are not the result of a heated imagination, nor the wild effusions of a disordered brain, but the genuine effects of God's Holy Spirit. There has, as yet, been no instance of any one professing godliness that has turned back, or dishonored his profession. But God only knoweth what may be in the future; and to us it belongeth to bow with reverence before him, giving thanks at the remembrance of his holiness.

CHAPTER XX.

An account of a Revival of Religion in DURHAM, CONN., in the year 1803. By the Rev. DAVID SMITH.

AT the time of my settlement, which was in August 1799, a general stupidity prevailed among the people in respect to religion. In the autumn following, I proposed to the church to appoint a conference, which should be attended once a fortnight, for the purpose of prayer and religious improvement. At the third meeting, if I rightly remember, a woman in middle life, was deeply impressed, and went home in great distress. Similar feelings were soon produced in her husband, and both were extremely anxious for their spiritual welfare. But a Sovereign God soon spake peace to their souls. Several instances of a similar kind occurred in the three succeeding years; and several additions were made to the church. But nothing very special appeared, until sometime in the latter part of the winter and spring of 1803. Then our meetings became crowded, and it became necessary to increase their number. In May, June, and July, they were very crowded and solemn. God was now in very deed among us, manifesting his sovereign power and grace in bringing down the lofty looks of man, and subduing the pride of the human heart. Some who were strongly opposed to the work at its commencement, and employed against it the shafts of ridicule, were brought to submit to the power of divine grace, and to embrace those truths which they before opposed.

From the time we began to attend religious conferences, which was in the autumn of 1799, till the awakening began in 1803, twelve were added to the church. From the fifth of March 1803, to the close of that year, forty persons came forward, and publicly professed the religion of Jesus. To this number twenty-three have since been added, making in the whole sixty-three, who may be considered fruits of this revival.

The feelings and sentiments entertained by the subjects of this work, may be learned from a few instances which I have selected.

One young lady, in giving an account of the exercises of her mind, after describing her distress under a sense of sinfulness and opposition of heart to God, writes thus:

' On the evening of the same day, I attended a conference meeting, which was solemn and edifying. Here new feelings occupied my breast. I thought I felt wholly resigned to the will of God, and that I could praise him, even were he to send me to hell. Since that evening, my feelings have been very different from what they ever were before. Every thing appears new. My Bible is quite a new book, and the doctrines of grace I cordially approve. I think I have reason to believe, that it was on the evening above mentioned, if ever, that God made me willing to accept salvation, and embrace the Saviour on the terms of the gospel. It is not in consequence of any thing that I have done, but from the boundless mercy and free grace of God, that he has been pleased to bring my soul out of the horrible pit and miry clay, and cause it to rest as I humbly hope, on the rock Christ Jesus."

Another in describing her distress of mind, and opposition of heart to God, writes thus:

"What to do, I knew not. If I went to my Bible for relief, I found none. If I attempted to pray, I found no satisfaction. All that I did, or ever had done, was sin. I found that I was entirely opposed to God and his wise decrees, and sometimes felt disposed to accuse him of partiality—that he was not so kind to me as to some others. At other times, I felt that I was the chief of sinners, and that it required a longer time for me to repent. I thought that if I could see my heart as it really was, I should be some better, and consequently that Christ would receive me. But alas, I was attempting to be my own Saviour. At length, I was brought to feel that I was utterly unable to save myself; that during my whole life, I had never done one act from a right motive; but that I had constantly been adding sin to sin. But in those distressing hours, God, I trust, compelled, or secretly constrained me to throw down the weapons of my rebellion, and to cast myself at Immanuel's feet, and to feel reconciled to the dispensations of his grace. This reconciliation, I think I realized, at a conference meeting on the evening of the 23d of June, 1803. That was the time, as I humbly trust, when God was pleased of his infinite mercy, to shed abroad his love in my broken heart. I saw such beauty and holiness in God as no tongue can describe. I wondered that I had never seen such a glorious God and precious Saviour before; and I was filled with astonishment that I was then out of hell."

Another instance which I would mention, was a woman about forty years of age. She gave this account of herself:

"I was one of that unhappy number, who depend on morality for salvation. I thought that if I lived a moral life, God would not be so unjust as to make me forever miserable. Thus I continued till I repeatedly heard the doctrine of election and divine decrees. I found that my heart was dreadfully opposed to such doctrines. I could not bear to think that I was in the hands of a Sovereign God. It was too mortifying to my proud heart to grant that he is the potter, and I the clay."

Such were her feelings for some time. On returning from meeting one Sabbath, being greatly irritated at the doctrines which she had heard, she rashly formed this resolution, that she would quit the public worship of God, and attend to her Bible only. Soon after she got home, she took her Bible and sat down. On opening the sacred volume, the first passage which engaged her attention was the following: "Moreover whom he did predestinate, them he also called; and whom he called, them he also justified; and whom he justified, them he also glorified." Several other passages of similar import occurred to her mind, and she immediately saw that the doctrines, with which she had been quarreling, were clearly contained in the Holy Scriptures, and that in opposing them, she had opposed God. This filled her with extreme distress, and she was impressed with the idea, that she was one of the non-elect, and consequently that she must be miserable forever. She saw that she was dead in trespasses and sins—that all her morality was of a selfish kind, and that she had never performed one act of duty acceptable to God. She remained in this situation not a long time before she received comfort, and was made to rejoice in the character and government of God. She has ever since been peculiarly attached to those doctrines, to which she had been most violently opposed.

A young man, now a member of Yale College, in stating his views and feelings, expressed himself thus:

"I began as I supposed, to reform my conduct, and live a better life. I attended on the outward means of religion, and was more strict on the Sabbath. But still I did not find that comfort in religion which I sought; for I found that I had no delight in holiness, to which my heart was opposed. If I asked advice of religious people, the answer would be *repent, and believe, and give up yourself to Christ.* But how to do this, I knew not. In this situation, I knew not what to do. My own works did me no good, but rather seemed to make me worse. I determined to abandon my self-dependence, and rely only on Christ for salvation. I remained not long in this situation. One evening as I was returning from meeting, if I am not deceived, I felt the love of the Saviour in my heart. I thought he was truly the one altogether lovely. I thought I was willing to own him for my prophet, priest and king. I now saw that if I was born into the kingdom of Christ, it was through the sovereign grace of God, and not for any thing that I had done."

I might mention a number of other instances very similar to those already described, but I forbear, and confine myself to one other, which is the most striking.

A man between 40 and 50 years of age, his wife having, a few weeks before, been hopefully made a subject of divine grace, had his attention called up by an extraordinary dream. The strongest convictions immediately ensued. His distress was so great, that he observed to a person present, that should he hold his finger in the candle, and let it burn off, it would be less than what he then endured. He felt his heart strongly opposed to God and to the methods of his grace. In this situation he remained several days, being almost, or quite in despair. He one day retired into the field, with little expectation of ever returning. He felt himself to be one of the greatest of sinners, and expected soon to plunge into eternal woe. While sitting in this situation, he seemed to feel a stroke on his back, at which he immediately started up, but did not discover from whence it came. This distress immediately left him, and the first object which attracted his attention was a bunch of flowers, which to him, appeared the most beautiful of any which he ever saw. He took them into his hand with a view to carry them to his wife ; and when he cast his eyes abroad upon the fields, to him the face of nature assumed a new appearance, and all the works of God were full of beauty beyond what he could describe. On his returning home, those who saw him immediately perceived in him a great alteration. He went out borne down with distress and sorrow, and returned full of joy. He now thinks that if he ever experienced a change of heart, it was at that time, though he then had not the most distant idea of any such thing. Such have been the wonderful effects of divine grace on the hearts of sinners. From the most obdurate enemies, God is able to form the most cordial friends.

CHAPTER XXI.

An account of a Revival of Religion in WASHINGTON, CONN., in the years 1803 and 1804. By the Rev. EBENEZER PORTER.

THOUGH this church has enjoyed a preached gospel, with very little interruption, since its formation, a period of sixty-four years, nothing that could properly be termed a revival of religion, had ever taken place till the present. In the vacancy immediately preceding my ordination, there was, in one part of the society, more than usual attention; and a number united with the church. In the three succeeding years, including 1799, twenty-three persons more were added. During the four next years, only ten persons made a public profession of religion. Death and removals were rapidly thinning our numbers; and there was room for solemn apprehension, that soon a solitary few would meet at the communion table; and our Zion be left to mourn that by multitudes her solemn feasts and her Sabbaths were forgotten. Though this people have long been accustomed to a decent and full attendance on public worship, and though as free, probably, as almost any other from open immoralities, it ought to be acknowledged with humility, that at the period above mentioned, the influence of vital religion among us was extremely low. Many hearts were locked up in impenetrable stupidity. Many families had no altar for God. Many parents seemed to behold their dear offspring going in the ways that lead to destruction, without uttering one warning, or offering one prayer for their eternal salvation. *Out* of the church, was to be seen a general carelessness. *In* it, a spirit of deep slumber; a want of discipline; want of active brotherly love; want of Christian watchfulness, faithfulness, prayerfulness; want of every thing, almost, but *cold, cold profession*. My heart aches at the remembrance, and trembles under the apprehension that such a season may return.

A glimmering hope of better things was enjoyed for a short time in the winter of 1801. A weekly church conference was attended regularly about two months, when it declined till it entirely ceased. The same unpleasant result attended every similar undertaking the winter following. After a few weeks, some other object engrossed the attention, and the conference was forgotten. At a leisure season, and on one of the finest evenings in the year, when it was to have been at my house, not an individual came. It seemed as though an offended God was about to seal us up, under the holy rebuke, "Sleep on now, and take your rest.———" That the only hope of self-destroying men, is the sovereign mercy of God, I had long believed, and often felt in some measure, but had never so deeply felt before. Means, however, were not to be neglected. For several years previous to this, endeavors had been used to interest the church in behalf of the rising generation. Early in the summer of 1802, special meetings were appointed for the youth; but not until the express approbation and support of the church had been engaged in favor of the object; as it was foreseen that without this, no permanent good would be effected. These meetings were attended every other week in the form of a *theological school.* At each meeting, a question, in the order of a system, was given, accompanied with an extempore lecture, or with some notice that a sermon would be adapted to the subject on the following Sabbath. When the latter course was taken, an unusual attention was apparent in the youth as well as in many others. At the meeting succeeding that on which the question was given, the papers that had been written by the youth, were received and read publicly. After a number of solemn, practical remarks on the last question, another was given in the same manner. From respect to the delicacy of the writers, their papers were received so as to have the author of each one unknown to every other. With the same precaution they were returned; having been reviewed at leisure, and such corrections or remarks as were thought necessary being made on them in writing. These meetings, begun with fair expectations, succeeded to to my joy and astonishment. They, in some degree, substituted solid improvement, for the ordinary levities of young people. They excited a relish for profitable conversation, reading and reflection. They furnished the mind with useful ideas, rendered the more permanent by the labor of acquiring them; and what is most important of all, they opened an avenue for the solemn influence of truth, by a divine blessing, to reach the conscience and the heart. A respectable number usually attended on the occasions; and twelve or fifteen wrote on the same question. It was surprising to witness the progress made by these, not only in correct writing, but in doctrinal knowledge. For three successive summers, these pleasant and profitable meetings were continued; when it was the will of a holy

God to suspend them, through my impaired health. To that will I desire to bow submissively, while I feel this allotment as the severest trial of my life.

Near the close of the summer 1803, things begun to wear a brighter aspect. Several persons became seriously impressed. At the request of six or eight brethren of the church, weekly conferences were revived. There was henceforth no more difficulty to maintain them. During the winter the operations of the divine Spirit were discernible in a part of the society. The church, which had appeared to languish as with a wasting hectic, put on the aspect of returning health. Through the next spring and summer, though thirteen had been added to Christ's visible family, we were still betwixt hope and fear. God's people longed for, rather than expected it. Scarcely did they dare to believe that so blessed a season was already begun; and that the day had indeed dawned which was to succeed a night of more than sixty years. In the autumn, the sun of righteousness arose upon us with healing and salvation in his wings. As in another valley of the Son of Hinnom, there was a great shaking. Dry bones, animated by the breath of the Almighty, stood up, new-born believers. Numbers, like the smitten Saul, were ready to say, "Lord, what wilt thou have us to do?" While the children of Zion, beheld with overflowing hearts, and with thankful tongues acknowledged, "this is the finger of God." The work was stamped conspicuously with the impress of its divine author; and its joyful effects evinced no other than the agency of Omnipotence. Every Sabbath exhibited the striking contrast betwixt a time of stupidity, and a time of attention, among a people. Many who had frequented the sanctuary from custom, or curiosity, unmoved by all that is joyful or alarming in the gospel; whose attention had been more occupied with a *new face* or a *new fashion*, than with the eternal interests of their own souls, were now in attitude of anxious and solemn inquirers, listening to the instructions of the pulpit. At conferences, the people collected as though they were awake and in earnest. Even those whom age and infirmity might well have excused, were often seen miles from home, at an evening meeting. On one of these occasions, the crowd which came together, reminded one of the assembly at Capernaum, when "there was not room to receive them, no, not so much as about the doors." Before the beginning of winter, the solemnity had extended to almost every part of the place. So manifestly was it the work of God, that opposition, however it might have rankled in the bosoms of individuals, was awed into silence. Many old professors, amidst the majesty and the glory of the scene, seemed unable to contain, and equally unable to express the wonder and joy of their hearts. In *them*, slumber at such a season, could hardly have been less than the lethargy of death. Thursday lectures, principally preached by neighboring ministers, were attended, for several months, with great solemnity and profit. A weekly prayer meeting was also set up, which is since devoted to a special remembrance of the rising generation, the first week in every month. During a winter, unusually severe, nothing could surpass the resolution with which numbers attended to be instructed in the way of salvation. From the extremity of the season, apprehensions were entertained for persons of delicate constitutions ; but the people were seldom, or never more healthy.

As the first fruit of this precious and memorable season, fifty-four persons have been added to the church ; none of whom, *blessed be God*, have, in their subsequent conduct, been left to discredit their holy profession. In consequence of such an accession, the situation of the church was thought to require that two new deacons should be chosen. This occasion, while it exhibited a prevailing, and very pleasing unanimity in the church, was rendered the more interesting, by a rare concurrence of circumstances. The vote of the brethren designated two young men to the office, twin brothers, very exactly resembling each other, having joined the church together about ten years before; and having married sisters, who are also now sisters in this church.

It would be more important to delineate particularly the nature and fruits of this work, did it not bear so strong affinity, in these respects, to the revivals once and again described heretofore in your Magazine. Without an exception, its special subjects were calm in their exercises; and embraced that system of religious sentiments commonly acknowledged, and received in our churches. Before this awakening, it was sometimes with difficulty that we could sing a sacramental hymn. After so many dear and promising youth, and among these, so respectable a portion of the singers, had been called into the church, our next communion left impressions in many bosoms which can never, never be effaced. Cold must have been the heart on that occasion not to have felt what words cannot express. The recollection of these scenes excite joy; but joy mingled with pain. Alas! that any, who are perishing with a mortal disease, should slight so fair an opportunity to find the great Physician, and the healing balm of the gospel. That season of special mercy is past. We have too many and too painful evidences that it is past. At least, a thousand precious immortal souls remain, whose situation it becomes not a fallible fellow creature to decide; but who, at present, do not profess to have any solid grounds of hope beyond the grave. O, that the God of mercy may vouchsafe his gracious and powerful presence to this dear flock; and that this time of solemn and sweet refreshing may be but the spring of a more prosperous summer, and a more glorious harvest.

From the commencement of this work to its visible decline, was more than eighteen months. One thing which it has impressed, more deeply than ever on my mind, is the benefit of religious conferences. These meetings, though frequent, seemed not at all to interfere with necessary temporal employments. An increased industry could easily redeem the time devoted to this purpose, from unprofitable or foolish pursuits. Such as have been the real and happy subjects of this work, and have so often met to pray, and praise, and converse, when they shall be numbered with the saints of the Most High in the glories of his everlasting kingdom, will doubtless remember, with transport, these small portions of time, big with eternal joy. In days like these, lowering with dark prospects over the church, and over the world, Christians, especially Christians who can meet in one half hour, most certainly ought not to live like strangers.

The religious instruction of children and youth, is another subject, the importance of which has been rendered more strikingly apparent in this revival. Of the number added to the church, about three-fourths had sprung from professing parents. Before this season, as is mentioned above, more than ordinary attention had been paid to the rising generation. Beside the meetings of the young people, the church, *as a church*, had appointed a catechising committee, to assist the pastor in teaching the children. These catechisings have been since regularly attended, during the summer season, between the services on every other Sabbath;

the children being classed according to their knowledge.*

The period from twelve to twenty, is eminently the learning and the forming age. Perhaps no other equal period so often determines the character for life, and the state for eternity. Still, this golden period is often spent, so as to be no better, or even worse than a blank. Little is learned but what requires the labor of a life to unlearn. Ought not something to be done, or at least, seriously attempted, for a reformation in this respect? While infidelity is searching out every avenue, for infusing its deadly poison into the minds of the young, is it not matter of surprise that their religious instruction should not have had more share in the thoughts, the conversation, the prayers of God's people! Do not the signs of the times summon ministers and Christians generally, to exertions more united, and more correspondent with an object of such acknowledged and immense importance? Surely it is no season for Zion's friends to count up

---

* In the fall of the year, there is an annual catechising, when every child that has attended the stated catechisings through the season, receives some religious tract, purchased with money drawn from the church treasury, and corresponding in value with the child's progress. The names of such as learn the catechism through, are also entered on the church records.

discouragements and to fold their hands in sloth, surrounded as they are, with such alarming proofs, that Zion's foes neither slumber nor sleep. Does not sin lie at the door of our churches? Is not one important end of infant baptism too much forgotten? If it is a grand design of this ordinance, "to draw the cares and prayers of the whole Christian church towards the rising generation, and their everlasting concerns; to hold them up perpetually before our eyes, and to fix them habitually upon our hearts," I apprehend that no subject of equal magnitude is so lamentably neglected.

CHAPTER XXII.

An account of a Revival of Religion in Canton, Conn., in the years 1805 and 1806. By the Rev. Jeremiah Hallock.

It pleased the Lord gloriously to visit this place, by the special influences of his Holy Spirit, in the latter part of 1798, and in the fore part of 1799. In this time, the drooping church was not a little quickened and comforted, and between seventy and eighty were added to it, an account of which was published in the first volume of the Magazine.

That day can never be forgotten by the church in this place; and to the praise of God be it spoken, the lapse of seven years has not weakened the faith of the candid beholder in the work of that day.

But by reason of deaths and removals, the church became considerably reduced, and inattention to divine things prevailed, and was increasing, especially among the youth, so that the things of religion began to wear a very gloomy appearance.

But in the early part of last June, one of the youth was visibly under serious impressions. This was soon attended with a solemn effect on the young people. It was not long before several others were awakened in the same neighborhood where the above-mentioned youth lived. And from this time the attention increased.

It seemed to operate like leaven, hid in three measures of meal. New instances of awakening often occurred.

The neighboring ministers, as well as some more remote, were very kind to visit us, and to preach to us. Indeed it seemed as if the Lord sent them. And almost every meeting was attended with some visible effect, until there were some instances of attention in almost every part of the parish. Lectures and conferences were frequent, and public religious meetings were full and serious. And this spiritual work appeared gradually to rise, for more than three months. The attention has been mostly among young people. It seemed as if God had fixed his eyes on the youth, though numbers of children have been seriously impressed; and there have also been some instances from thirty to sixty.

Of the subjects of this work, the largest proportion are females. Towards thirty have obtained hopes. Fifteen have joined the church, and others are expected to come forward, and subscribe with their hands unto the Lord. As when the cry was made, " Behold the bridegroom cometh," the virgins arose and trimmed their lamps, this has been a day of alarm to the church. They appeared to be aroused in some measure from their formal state into which even the wise are so apt to fall while the bridegroom tarries. Some were ready to cry, Our lamps are gone out.

Having noticed these things concerning the beginning and progress of this revival, I shall add, as a specimen of the work, the relation of two youth, as written by themselves to a friend. The first writes thus :

" Dear Sir—The following lines are a short sketch of what, I hope, the great Sovereign of the Universe has been pleased to do for me, a poor, unworthy sinner. Time has wafted me through the days of childhood, perhaps as thoughtless of God, and insensible of eternity, as any one can be. Whenever I was aroused to think on death and judgment, I would silence the voice of conscience, and say, I could not cherish such gloomy thoughts when I was in health and prosperity; little thinking that my soul was out of health. Therefore I abandoned these thoughts, which ought to have been most dear to me. But, blessed be God, he has spared my life until now, and, as I hope, made me a living monument to adore his glorious name.

"My mind first began to be seriously impressed last July, at the funeral of Mrs. D. C. I followed the breathless body to the silent mansions of the dead, little thinking it was a lesson for me to read. I considered myself an uninterested beholder. But when I saw the corpse laid in the grave, the thought struck my mind, will this suffice? Will the grave now shut its mouth, and say, enough? The answer was ready; no, it will not, but it will soon claim me in spite of all my efforts. But when I looked beyond the grave, eternity appeared still more awful. These words seemed to be directed to me, 'What meanest thou, O sleeper? Arise, and call upon thy God.'

"This led me to look into my polluted heart, where I found nothing but sin and guilt, which were pressing me down into the pit of wo and misery. And my days that were past, were irrecoverably gone forever. But a thousand hurrying thoughts of the world, seemed to bear me away from these feelings; and many times did I put on the veil of cheerfulness, when I had an aching heart within, for fear of the ridicule of the thoughtless part of mankind, who have got to stand at the tribunal of God, as well as myself.

"Thus my days were spent until about the middle of September, when the horrors of hell appeared before me, unavoidable. I felt myself to be a sinner, and exposed to the wrath of God, who was continually saying, 'Vengeance is mine, I will repay.' In vain I sought relief from the Bible. Every line seemed to condemn me. I thought I was doing all I could to purchase happiness, and my reading, praying, sighs and moans were in such earnest, I thought I should move heaven to pity me. But all was in vain, it was in such a selfish manner. And I thought I was unjustly bound with the cords of disquietude, and doomed to eat the bread of sorrow, while many of my young companions could triumph over death and the grave, and sing, 'Thy love, O Jesus, is the theme;' but I was unheard and unanswered, and left to wear out my hours in grief alone. This I thought was unjust, and my heart rose in dreadful opposition against God. Oh, how hard is the human heart. If it had the power, it would dethrone the Almighty. But blessed be God, the power is in his own hands.

"I remained in this sorrowful situation several days, seeking relief, but refusing the precious balm of Gilead. A certain Monday in this month was a most trying day to me. It seemed as if the whole universe gazed, with an eye of contempt, on its sinful, wretched inhabitants. But O, the following Wednesday! May that precious day never be erased from my memory—the day, as I hope, in which God met my poor, perishing soul. Having taken up the Hartford selection of hymns, I began to read the 274th—

> 'Cheer up, my soul, there is a mercy-seat,
>   Sprinkled with blood, where Jesus answers prayer;
> There humbly cast thyself beneath his feet,
>   For never needy sinner perished there.'

And truly, I then said to myself, who can wish for a higher seat, than at the feet of Sovereign mercy? And my heart was now ready to thank God that I was in his hands. And O, how astonishing it was, that his mercy was extended even to me, who had been contending with him all my days; refusing all his blessed calls and invitations, trampling under foot his dear Son, who had spilt his precious blood upon the cross for me, and yet not one moment had I spent in his service. Now my heart could join with the psalmist in saying, 'O come and let us worship, and bow down, let us kneel before the Lord our Maker.' Also, 'Who can utter the mighty acts of the Lord, who can show forth all his praise?' His perfections were visible in the whole creation. A sermon was preached that afternoon from Solomon's song, chap. 4: 5, 8, 'Come with me from Lebanon, my spouse,' &c. These appeared to be in reality Christ's words, and the sermon was sweet to my soul, through the whole exercise. I felt as if my soul was feasted on the food of eternal life, which God had prepared for all who serve him in spirit and in truth. And if I do not labor under a great mistake, it is my desire to serve God, and I can trust my all with him and rely upon his Word. I hope I have enjoyed the presence of God, most of the time, but sometimes, through my own negligence, and falling so far short of the duty which I owe him, I am left to lament the withdrawing of his smiles, and to trying doubts. But I must conclude by asking your prayers, sir, and the prayers of all God's children, that I may be kept from the snares with which I am surrounded, in this evil world, and that I may be preserved through the faith of Jesus unto death. Then,

> 'Filled with delight, my raptured soul
> Can here no longer stay;
> Though Jordan's waves around me roll,
> Fearless I'd launch away.'"

The second writes in the following words:

"Dear Sir—I shall now, as enabled, state to you some of the recent dealings of God with my soul. My mind began to be impressed with a sense of my sins, and consequent danger, in the beginning of last April. But the great and general stupidity with which I was then surrounded, together with the fear of becoming an object of derision, caused me to conceal my distress until the beginning of June, when it rose to such a height, that I found concealment impossible. For a certain period, during two or three weeks, the black catalogue of the sins of my whole life appeared to be set in order before my eyes, accompanied with a deep sense of my being in the hands of a holy, sin-hating God, and entirely at his disposal.

"It seemed as though nature would sometimes sink under the pressure; but He who thus laid his hand on me, was still my support. In July, when the attention to religion had become considerable, I began to find that I had not only a wicked heart, but that it was entirely selfish, and filled with the most dreadful and daring opposition to God; and that selfishness had been, and still was, the great moving principle of all my actions. This put me to a great stand. My inquiry now was with more anxiety than ever, "What must I do to be saved?" I now saw that the prayers of the wicked are an abomination unto the Lord. Yet I was told that prayer was a duty incumbent upon me notwithstanding my own sinfulness, and that I ought to pray with a penitent heart. This was what I could not bear, and I found myself actually at war with God Almighty. It appeared to me that annihilation would be far preferable to the situation in which I then was. I would gladly have changed condition with the very stones in the street, and frequently looked with envy on the meanest reptiles of the earth.

"Whenever I opened my Bible, I found it filled with threatenings against me. I found also that it demanded true and unfeigned submission to God, as the only condition on which salvation would be granted. I attended many meetings, but they only served to augment my distress, and if possible to increase my opposition. For several weeks, I almost entirely relinquished business, and spent my time principally in walking in my chamber. Whenever I heard of any person's obtaining a hope, it was like adding fuel to the fire. My heart rose against it, and accused God of exercising partiality with his creatures, not considering that he had a right to do what he would with his own.

"These exercises continued until August, when the terrors of hell seemed to compass me about. From Tuesday, the 6th, to Wednesday, the 14th, it appeared to me that I stood on the very confines of destruction, and was permitted to look into the eternal world. Death and judgment were now most solemn realities, and they so overwhelmed me that I was many times ready to sink into despair, and give up all hope of ever obtaining mercy.

> 'Then O, how vain appeared
> All things beneath the sky,
> Like visions past, like flowers that blow,
> When wintry storms are nigh.'

But it pleased a great and merciful God not to keep me long in this painful situation. On

Wednesday, the 14th of August, I attended a lecture, when a sermon was preached from John 4: 49—'The nobleman saith unto him, sir, come down, ere my child die.' Upon hearing these words and their explanation, I found my heart glowing with the most ardent love toward the Saviour. He appeared to be the chiefest among ten thousand, and altogether lovely—every way suited to my necessities. Tears flowed without control. The language of my heart was, O, my dear Saviour, come, and take an everlasting possession of my soul. I bid thee a hearty welcome to my heart, and would lie low at thy feet forever. My emotions were so great that I found it difficult to keep from immediately kneeling upon the floor, and extending my arms where I then was, in the meeting-house. I had no idea that this was conversion. I returned home, and without mentioning any thing to the family, retired to rest as usual. And here again I found my soul drawn forth in the most affectionate desires after the Saviour. I found those beautiful lines in Dr. Watts' versification applicable to what I then felt:

' My flesh lay resting on my bed,
My soul arose on high.'

With my mind composed to the most perfect

peace, I now went to sleep. On awaking in the morning, I concluded that I had become entirely stupid, and accordingly made several attempts to bring on my former distress. But this I found was impossible. I then resolved to walk out, and reflect on the exercises of the day and evening preceding. But instead of this, the character of God himself now came into view, and filled my soul with joy, love, and gratitude, wonder and admiration, to that degree that bodily strength failed; and for some minutes, I became almost insensible to surrounding objects. Upon recovering myself, I found that every thing around me wore a new aspect. The glory of God appeared to be visible in every part of creation. I saw the hills, mountains and fields, all lying beneath the omniscient eye of God, and answering the great end for which they were created, the glory of God. And now the thought occurred, shall man, who is the noblest part of creation, be silent? This was an amazing thought. I stood like one astonished at myself. Why had I never thought of this before? I now saw that I had indeed been willfully blind, and that it would have been just in God, had he left me to my own chosen way. I now began to imagine that this might be conversion. But I had many doubts about it, because that, during all these exercises, I had strangely forgotten myself. These doubts were, however, soon removed, when I found that I was entirely willing that God should dispose of me for time and eternity, as he saw best, and most for his glory. And O, what heartfelt joy did it give me to reflect that I was in the hands of God. It was like an anchor to my soul.

"The Bible, religious meetings, and the duties of the closet, became the food of my soul. The latter becomes every day more and more precious to me. How does my heart frequently expand with rapture while I am praying for the advancement of the Redeemer's kingdom. When gloom and darkness fill my mind, as is sometimes the case, in consequence of the remaining sinfulness of my heart, I find that the thought that God's kingdom is eternal, and stands secure, generally removes the cloud. This, sir, is, according to my best recollection, a short sketch of what I have, through the goodness of God, been made to experience. I would now conclude by asking your prayers for me, that I may not be left to dishonor God in the profession which I have made."

Having given the foregoing account of the sovereign and most merciful dealings of the Lord towards us, his sinful and unworthy creatures, I shall close by only observing, that days of attention are not trifling days, but most solemn and serious to all. It becometh those that are left, to tremble; and such as hope, not to be high-minded, but to fear lest after all, they should come out withered branches, only fit for the fire, to the dishonor of Christ, the grief of Zion, and their own shame.

CHAPTER XXIII.

An account of a Revival of Religion in HARWINTON, CONN., in the years 1805, and 1806. By the Rev. JOSHUA WILLIAMS.

THE first appearance of this work was about the middle of September 1805, nearly seven years from the beginning of that in 1799. Its progress was very rapid, attended with marks of divine sovereignty. In the course of four or five weeks after its first appearance, fourteen or fifteen were brought to entertain a joyful, yet humble hope of their conversion, from a state of enmity, to a state of reconciliation to God. In the beginning of October occurred an instance, which became, by the blessing of God, a powerful means of bringing conviction home to the consciences of others; and many became deeply impressed with a sense of the deceitfulness and desperate wickedness of the heart, and of the awful displeasure of a holy God against sin. After the period before mentioned, the work seemed to be suspended for nearly four weeks.

In the meantime, instances of convictions, and the power of them, rather increased, by which God seemed to be giving testimony to the reality and sovereignty of his grace, showing that it is his peculiar work to wound and to heal, to convict of sin, and to afford consolation to the sin-sick soul. It is to be observed, that though twenty or thirty persons were in great distress of mind, during the apparent suspension of the work; yet there is no ground to believe that relief was sent, during the whole period, to more than one soul. But soon after this, many were favored with precious relief and real comfort in view of the Lord Jesus Christ, and his ability to save; and all in the way of exercising cordial submission (as we have reason to hope,) to God in Christ. Some, however, remained in great distress for many weeks, till animal nature, in some cases, seemed to be nearly exhausted. To such the revelation of Jesus Christ as the glory of God, and the suitable resting place of souls, was as life from the dead.

The work continued to make progress, without very sensible abatement, for nearly six months; in which time numbers were hopefully converted, and such visible tokens of divine grace, and infinite and sovereign love were exhibited, as gave abundant occasion for the warmest thanksgiving, "and the children of Zion were made joyful in their king," who appeared in his glory to build it up.

Several things occurred besides the suspense already mentioned, to manifest the divine sovereignty of this work. While some well educated, moral, and apparently religious young people, who had previously considered religion to be important, were continued under the pains of a wounded and comfortless spirit for fifty or sixty days; others who had scarcely had one realizing thought of eternity, were unexpectedly arrested, and in a few days became joyful subjects of religous hope.

At a time when poisonous sentiments are disseminated with great industry, and in the most alluring manner, there is no reason to wonder, if many should be induced to neglect public worship, and other means of grace, and become, as is usual in such cases, excessively bitter in their minds, if not in their speech, against any special work of God's Spirit. But, to the praise of rich and glorious grace, be it said, some of this class have been arrested, and if we may judge from their uniform testimony, humbled and changed. Instances of this kind have occurred in such peculiar circumstances, as to set at defiance every attempt to assign any sufficient cause, but that of the good pleasure and power of God. Indeed, no sensible person, that would fairly look at the case, let his feelings of heart be what they might, could afterwards venture to assign any other cause.

The wicked heart seemed to be overawed by the majesty and the sovereignty of the work: and to appear an opposer, was to appear to be led, not by rational views of things, but by the spirit which actuated the Jews in their opposition to the work of God, when Paul and Barnabas were preaching successfully at Antioch. Acts 13: 45.

At this time, several, who had been exceedingly prejudiced against experimental religion, and who had, principally on that account, refused to worship with us, were signally affected by divine truth, and they have come, and as experienced Christians who love that truth which they once derided, have joined in communion with this church. One instance I will mention. A woman who had not attended our meetings, and scarcely any other for almost seven years, one who was remarkably opposed to the idea of a revival, was, in the very act of ridiculing a sister that was in some measure impressed, *pricked in the heart;* and after some violent, but ineffectual attempts to remove or conceal her emotions, she was obliged to submit in a visible manner to convictions of a very distressing kind. In consequence she was led to attend with great earnestness and anxiety of soul, upon those means against which she once had an obstinate prejudice. And in short, she has a very evident change of views and character. She has been admitted into the church as a new born child of God, and none can rationally attribute her experience to delusion, or to any power short of that which is almighty.

The Sovereignty and power of God in this gracious work, appear not only in respect to the persons who become the subjects of it, but also in respect to their ages. Though a few were of middle age, yet generally they were between the age of thirteen and twenty-five. Some, however, were much older. To one particular case I think I may invite attention. It is that of an old lady now deceased, who through infirmity of body was not able to attend public worship, and scarcely to go to a neighbor's for twelve or fifteen years. There is reason to hope that this woman experienced a saving change of heart, when she wanted but a few days of being four score and eight years old. She was duly examined for admission into the church, was approved and propounded; but the wise disposer of all events was pleased to take her away before she could be regularly admitted. She died in a fit. In her last day, when from all appearances there was good ground for believing that she had the use of her reason, though unable to speak, she gave tokens, which were understood to be decided manifestations of her faith and confidence in God.

If any wish to be informed of the views, exercises and feelings of the subjects of the present work, it may be observed that they correspond, in nature and kind, with those of 1799, which are narrated in the first volume of the Magazine. To that and other narratives, the writer refers the reader. But although they thus in general correspond, yet in several respects there is a difference. That was principally among people from twenty-five to forty-five years of age.

This is mostly among those who are under twenty-five.

Convictions have at this time been generally more evidential of sovereignty and power. This is singular indeed; for from what had taken place before, among the middle aged, it might have been expected that there would be less evidence of this, and more of the influence of example and persuasion; and this undoubtedly would have been the case, had it been of men. But if it would not swell this narrative too much, it might be made to appear to all, that even in the religious families to which reference will presently be made, the evidence is decisive, that though God works in love and covenant faithfulness, yet it is when and where, and by what means he pleases.

Convictions too have been at this time more pungent and severe, and of a greater variety as to their duration previous to their relief. There have been more instances out of the common way. Their eyes and countenances were remarkably fixed, during the time of religious worship and at other times, and it seemed that nothing could be able to divert their attention from the great concerns of the soul. A few appeared to be so far overcome, as, at times, to be scarcely able to stand; but our assemblies were always remarkably quiet and still.

Again the hopeful converts have seemed to have at an earlier period, an acquaintance with the plague of their own hearts, and to have been made more painfully sensible of the remaining corruption within them, in consequence of which, several have suffered many days of distressing darkness after they had good reason to hope they should be saved. For, (as I suppose is the case with all Christians,) the hope of being forever in heaven, was not sufficient to comfort them, while so much imperfection remained in them.

Like the former, this awakening has extended into almost every part of the society, but the converts are not so numerous. In that, there were about one hundred and forty for whom we had reason to entertain hope. The number now is seventy-five.

Further—It deserves to be remarked that the greater part of the hopeful converts, yea, as many as nine out of ten, if I am not greatly deceived, are the children of religious parents, or persons who lived in pious and praying families. This seems to be a great encouragement to Christian parents ; and may I be permitted to observe, that usually the faithful exertions of pious parents are crowned with success. Their instructions are not all in vain. Though at times, they may nearly lose all hope, and their tenderest exertions seem only to make their children sin the more ; yet great is the benefit of persevering diligence ; and most generally it proves in the end successful. It ought, however, to be noticed that this is not always the case. To abase the pride of men, and to show that regeneration is not the result of religious education alone ; we find that a sovereign God is pleased by his Holy Spirit, to enter some prayerless and irreligious families, and one or more in them is made and kept a shining monument of his grace, while others, in the same family only see, and scoff, and perish. For the same purpose also, we find in a religious family, one or more, and perhaps such as the world esteem the brightest, left totally callous and insensible—*dead in trespasses and sins*, while the showers of divine love bring life and saving health to others. This is an awful distribution of divine grace, and the insensible in religious families have occasion to tremble, and immediately set themselves to work out their salvation, lest like the Jews of old, they shall at last find the dreadful portion of beholding their near relatives in the kingdom of God, and they themselves cast out.

In the former awakening it was observed that the subjects of it being principally heads of families, cast a delightful aspect on the rising generation; and now with pleasure we record that many of the late converts are the children of those who then introduced family instruction and prayer. In the month of October one was added to the church. In December four, and in January three. Almost all of these were considered as subjects of regenerating grace previous to this revival; and, in this, were brought to a stronger and more comfortable hope. On the second Sabbath of March, 1806, twenty-two made a profession of religion. In May, fourteen, in July, four, in August, six, and a number since, making the whole number sixty-two.

To close, I hope it will not appear arrogant to say, surely the members of this church, together with their pastor and the society, ought humbly and affectionately to acknowledge that they have very abundant reason for the liveliest exercise of gratitude and praise; and forever to bless the Lord of Hosts for such wonderful and repeated tokens of his mercy, and also continually to sing Alleluia. Amen.

P. S. Having mentioned in the foregoing narrative, that an instance occurred which became a powerful means of bringing home conviction to the consciences of others; I subjoin a few particulars respecting it. It is the case of a young woman of a respectable family, whose character from her earliest childhood, was uncommonly mild and good. She was less than fourteen years of age. As soon as she was capable, she was taught to pray; and when she was able to read, she was given to understand that it was a duty to read the Scriptures as a part of devotion. This she did, almost daily, for a number of years. To be short, she was viewed by all her acquaintance, young and old, as one of the most moral and religious of her age that could be found. Indeed she thought herself to be truly religious, and the thought of dying gave her no great uneasiness, for she supposed she should go to eternal blessedness;

and perhaps had she died, no one of her friends would have doubted of it. Soon after the awakening began, she felt a little more engaged, but felt nothing very impressive till the beginning of October, when she was informed of the conviction and exercises of an intimate friend, who a little before, had been brought, it is hoped, to find rest in Jesus Christ. This, with some observations at a conference meeting the same evening, were blessed to convince her that she had wholly mistaken the nature of the Christian religion ; and the conviction was so clear and pungent, that her distress was very visible. It continued several days, in one of which I called and found her, to appearance, as complete a picture of forlorn distress as I could remember to have seen. Affected with her case, I asked her what was the matter? She answered, "O sir, I have read the Bible in such a manner—and I have tried to pray, but knew not what I was about." By these words, she meant to communicate to me, as I understood by subsequent conversation, the sense she had of the great wickedness of reading the Bible in a heedless and cursory manner, and also of having attempted to pray from selfish motives and with a heart not filled with reverence and knowledge of God. It appeared to me very plainly, that her conduct had been so unexceptionable, that her awakened conscience could fix on no guilt but the selfishness and irreverence which had attended her religious devotions. From this alone she seemed to be convinced of the exceeding depravity of the heart, and of the absolute necessity of being born again; nor could any of the overtures of free mercy in the gospel, afford her relief, as long as she was unrenewed. She remained in great distress of mind for two days more, one of which was the Sabbath; when her mates, and many of the young people had an opportunity to see her. On Sabbath evening she experienced relief. Her great burden was removed, at which time she concluded that for her great obstinacy and abuse of mercy, God had left her to be sealed up to final destruction. Under this impression, she was led to take a view of God's government, and not long after said, with great solemnity and sweet simplicity, "I am losing all my impressions, and must perish; but it seems to me it is no matter what becomes of me, if God may be glorified." Soon after she opened the Bible, and read and commented on some passages to the pleasing surprise of those that were present, among whom I was one. She also read some hymns, with such feeling emphasis and rejoicing, that it was good to hear. After this she said, "I am in a dreadful condition, but joy will come." Having paused a while with a fixed countenance, she turned to me and asked if God did not often restrain people. I told her he did; and to give her a full sight of the human heart, I turned her to the latter part of the first chapter of Romans. Having read about half of it she exclaimed in the same artless simplicity, "what awful creatures we are." And after reading the remainder, she said, "there is room enough for humility, but no reason for us to be proud." After this I pointed her to the account in Galatians 5, and then to that in Corinthians, where the Apostle, after mentioning the dreadful crimes of sinners, adds, "and such were some of you; but ye are washed," &c. It was upon reading this, that she began to hope that possibly she might be saved by Jesus Christ.

This case did so eminently show the necessity of a change of heart in all, that it seemed to carry irresistible conviction to many; for they were led to reflect that if one so unexceptionable in her life, and so apparently religious, needed a new heart, and was in such distress without it, what must become of them, who, in comparison with her, had no religion at all. The case, indeed, was used for this purpose, and it is believed not altogether in vain. Soon many became convinced that the carnal mind, which was naturally within them, was enmity to God, and they were brought to view themselves, and the law of God, in a light vastly different from any that they had before.

CHAPTER XXIV.

An account of a Revival of Religion in South Britain, Conn., in the year 1812. By the Rev. Bennet Tyler.

[First published in the Panoplist.]

The first favorable appearances which gave us reason to hope that the Lord was about to visit us with the effusions of his Spirit, were discoverable early in the spring of 1812. During the preceding winter, it had been a time of great stupidity. The wise and the foolish appeared to be slumbering together. Meetings for religious conference and prayer, which for five years previous had been statedly attended, so far declined, that at the commencement of the winter, they were entirely discontinued. Our youth were remarkably thoughtless, and in some instances, began to be dissipated. Although the people generally paid constant and decent attention to public worship on the Sabbath; yet there was but very little of the life and power of religion manifested even among professors of religion.

Such was the state of things among us, till

about the beginning of the month of March, when the minds of a few members of the church in different parts of the society, were unusually impressed with a sense of our deplorable condition. About eight or ten pious persons, as I have since learnt, had very similar impressions, almost at the same time, each one being ignorant of the feelings of the rest. They were led deeply to humble themselves before God for their past backslidings, and earnestly to implore the reviving influences of the Holy Spirit.

Shortly after this, it was proposed to the church to set apart a day for fasting and prayer; partly on account of the distressing and mortal sickness which prevailed in some neighboring towns; but more especially on account of the great stupidity which prevailed among ourselves. A day was accordingly appointed, and to our great surprise, a larger congregation assembled than had been witnessed for a considerable time previous on the Sabbath. A prayer meeting was attended in the forenoon, which was very solemn. A sermon was preached in the afternoon, and another in the evening, by two ministers from abroad. An unusual attention and solemnity were visible throughout the assembly; and from that time forward, our congregations on the Sabbath assumed a new aspect.

About this time, a little circle of Christians set up a weekly prayer meeting, for the express purpose of supplicating the influences of the Holy Spirit. This meeting will never be forgotten by those who attended it. At these seasons, there were special tokens of the divine presence, and such wrestlings in prayer, as are, perhaps, rarely realized. The joys experienced by this little circle of praying people, were such as a stranger intermeddleth not with. They were precious foretastes of joys to be realized in a better world. Not long after this prayer meeting was set up, a public weekly conference was also instituted, which was crowded and solemn. In the meantime, an increasing attention and solemnity were visible in the congregation on the Sabbath.

Such was the state of things among us in the early part of the month of April; and although no persons were then known to be under special awakenings, yet we were led to hope that the Lord had mercy in store for us. Several pious persons were anxiously waiting for the consolation of Israel. They watched, with trembling hope, every motion of the little cloud which they discovered rising above the horizon; and they felt that confidence in the promises of God, which usually attends a spirit of prayer. It was not long before their hopes began to be realized. Four or five persons, in different parts of the parish, were awakened to a sense of their sin and danger, and began to inquire what they should do to be saved. These fresh tokens of the divine presence added new courage to those who had been praying and waiting for the blessing, and inspired them with strong expectations that their prayers were soon to be answered. But it was necessary that their faith and patience should be tried, that they might be the more fully prepared to give God the glory. For several weeks things remained stationary. The cloud which had been rising, and which promised a refreshing shower, appeared to stop. No new instances of conviction occurred. It was a time of trembling anxiety, and awful suspense. During the month of May, however, those who had been first awakened, obtained a hope of an interest in Christ, and some others were found to be under serious impressions. A more fervent spirit of prayer was poured out upon the members of the church, and in the latter part of June, the rain of divine influences descended in every part of the parish, like a mighty shower. Great numbers were awakened, and through the month of July, scarcely a day passed which will not be remembered as the spiritual birth-day of some one or more souls, who, as we trust, have been born of God. As many as forty, in the course of that month, obtained a hope of a saving interest in the Redeemer.

The scenes which were now passing before us cannot be described, nor can they be conceived of but by those who have witnessed scenes of a similar nature. The eyes of God's people sparkled with joy inexpressible, while the countenances of sinners were depicted with distress and horror. The things of eternity were now regarded as realities of infinite moment. From the gray-headed sinner to the little child, the question was daily asked, "What must I do to be saved?" Religion was now the great theme of discourse. In the family, in the street, in the field, and in the shop, it engrossed almost the whole conversation.

At this time, it is believed, the whole congregation were more or less impressed. Satan seemed to be bound for a little season, and all opposition was silenced. Opposers stood aghast.

They beheld, and wondered, and like the magicians of Egypt, were constrained to confess, "This is the finger of God." Several who had been open revilers, were arrested, and like the persecuting Saul of Tarsus were brought to espouse that cause which they had attempted to destroy.

Religious meetings were very frequently attended, and although it was the most busy season of the year, they were generally crowded. A very considerable congregation might, at any time, be collected upon the shortest notice. So great was the desire of the people to obtain religious instruction, that not unfrequently persons have been seen three and four miles from home, at an evening conference. But although the attention was so great, there was very little appearance of enthusiasm. Convictions, though, in many instances, deep and pungent, appeared to be rational. The utmost decorum prevailed in our meetings. There were no outcryings—no bodily agitations—but a solemn, awful stillness, which indicated the special presence of God. No attempts were made to work upon the passions and imaginations of the people; but the naked truths of the gospel were exhibited to their view, and pressed upon their consciences. The doctrines particularly insisted on, were the entire depravity of the human heart, the necessity of regeneration by the special influences of the Holy Spirit, justification by faith alone in the merits of a divine Saviour, and the sovereignty of God in the government of the world, and in the dispensations of his grace. These, together with the doctrines intimately connected with them, appeared to be the power of God unto salvation.

The number of those who have manifested a hope that they have passed from death unto life, since the revival commenced, is not far from eighty. That all of these will hold out to the end, is more than we can rationally expect; and indeed, some already give us too much reason to fear that they were no more than stony-ground hearers. But with few exceptions, they appear yet to bring forth fruit meet for repentance. Forty-eight have been added to the church. Three more stand propounded, and several others are expected soon to present themselves as candidates for admission.

The subjects of this work are of all ages, from nine years old to sixty. The largest number, however, is among the young. It is peculiarly interesting to witness the change which has taken place among the rising generation. Many who, eighteen months ago, were remarkably thoughtless, and some of them openly vicious, are now sober and discreet in their behavior, and appear to be growing fast in Christian knowledge. They have renounced the sinful vanities by which youth are apt to be fascinated, and have found from experience that wisdom's ways are ways of pleasantness, and that all her paths are peace.

In the previous external character of those who have been awakened and hopefully converted, there was a great diversity. Some were persons of exemplary morals, and constant attendants on the means of grace. Others were immoral in their conduct, deistical in their sentiments, regardless of the institutions of the gospel, and open revilers of the Christian religion. But by far the greatest proportion were persons who in early life had been dedicated to God, and who had enjoyed the privilege of a religious education. Thus while God has strikingly displayed his sovereignty, he has also remembered his covenant, and shown himself to be faithful to his promises.

The exercises of those who give evidence of having experienced a saving change, though essentially the same in all, have been circumstantially different in different persons. There was a great difference in persons under conviction, both as to the duration and pungency of their convictions. Some were distressed for months. Others obtained relief in a few weeks, and some in a few days after their first impressions. In many cases, convictions were very distressing. I have seen men in middle life, men of great natural fortitude, so borne down with a sense of guilt, that their burden seemed scarcely supportable. In others, though their convictions appeared to be equally genuine, they were not attended with that extreme distress. In most the work of conviction was gradual in its progress, though in some, much more rapid than in others. They were first awakened to a sense of their danger, and excited to make exertions to obtain salvation. They endeavored to recommend themselves to God by their abundant duties ; but as they came to see more of the nature of the divine law, they found that all their services were radically defective, and that so far from procuring the favor of God, they became more and more obnoxious to his wrath. In this way they were led to a sight of the total corruption of their hearts ; and it was not unusual for them to be troubled with dreadful heart-risings against the character and government of God, and against the requirements and threatenings of his law. They found that the carnal mind is indeed enmity against God. Thus they were brought to see their utterly lost state by nature, and their entire dependence on the sovereign and distinguishing mercy of God. While in this situation, their distress of mind was often great beyond description. But this was usually soon followed by joy and peace in believing.

When they obtained relief, their views of divine things appeared to be entirely changed, though the views of some were much more clear than those of others. The character of God as revealed in the Scriptures, against which they had felt great opposition, now appeared amiable. They could rejoice that just such a being was on the throne of the universe, and that he would dispose of all things, even of themselves, according to his sovereign pleasure. This seemed to be the language of their hearts— "Here are we, Lord, vile, unworthy, hell-deserving sinners, do with us as seemeth good in thy sight. If we are lost, it is just what we deserve. If we are saved, it will be all of grace ; and to

thy great name shall be given all the glory."
The law of God now appeared reasonable in all
its requirements, and righteous in its penalty.
In the character and offices of Christ as a
divine Saviour, they discovered a beauty and a
glory, of which before they had no conception.
They saw him to be just such a Saviour as they
needed. He was, therefore, precious to them,
and regarded as the chiefest among ten thous-
and, and altogether lovely. The Bible appeared
to them to be a new book. They found it a
rich treasury of precious instruction. The doctrines of grace, to which they had felt great
opposition, they cordially embraced. They felt
them to be the sincere milk of the Word, which
furnished them with spiritual nourishment.
They felt a peculiar love and attachment to the
people of God; and in the duties of religion
they experienced a satisfaction with which they
were before totally unacquainted. Concerning
the consolations of religion, they were ready to
say with the queen of Sheba, when she had
surveyed the glory of Solomon's kingdom, "It
was indeed a true report which we had heard of
these things, but lo! the half was not told us."

The above is but an imperfect sketch of what
we have been permitted to witness. *Truly the*

Lord hath done great things for us, whereof we are glad; and to his name be ascribed all the glory. O that men would praise the Lord for his goodness, and for his wonderful works to the children of men.

CHAPTER XXV.

An account of a Revival of Religion in BRIDPORT, VT., in the years 1813 and 1814. By the Rev. INCREASE GRAVES.

[First published in the Adviser, or Vermont Evangelical Magazine.]

THE attention to religion in this town, began in February, 1813. It commenced during that terrible sickness, which spread through this part of the country, and swept such numbers to the grave. About forty-four persons in the town died of that destructive malady. This was an alarming providence, and it is not surprising that it inspired some with concern for their souls.

During the summer previous, there were several remarkable instances of persons dying in the triumph of faith. To these, the attention of the people was directed, and much was said concerning the blessedness of dying in the Lord. Soon after, that dreadful sickness prevailed, and a number of those who died, departed in deplorable stupidity, although they had ample ground

BRIDPORT, VT. 363

for alarm. The contrast was not only seen, but viewed with astonishment.

The sickness above alluded to, appears to have been employed by Divine Providence to begin the great and good work, which lasted almost two years from its commencement; and even now, it is a time of much seriousness. Nothing, however, occurred which attracted public notice, till the latter part of the summer, when three persons came forward to unite with the church, two encouraged by a former, and one by a recent hope. At a much earlier period, indeed, appearances were such that I was ready to hope that God had visited us in mercy. But when, as the spring advanced, the conferences, which had been attended during the week, were discontinued, because the evenings became too short to admit of their being then held, and no others were maintained, except those on the afternoon of the Sabbath, the indications of a revival disappeared. My hopes sunk, and I thought that I had at no time known the church in a more languid and unpromising state. Political controversy ran high, and political topics engrossed general attention. On the Sabbath, as I was returning to the meeting-house for the afternoon service, I discovered clusters discussing political subjects with a considerable degree of warmth. I was astonished that any part of the Sabbath should be spent in a manner so useless and culpable, and that this should be done by professed Christians, instead of being engaged in social or secret prayer for their minister and for the prosperity of religion. Such were my feelings, that I resolved that at the coming church meeting, which was on Friday of the same week, I would bring the subject forward. I accordingly stated to the church my views of the impropriety of the practice, and urged them to renounce it, and to consecrate the Sabbath exclusively to religion. To this the church agreed, and also, that during the twilight of every Saturday evening, they would hold a concert of prayer. This agreement was faithfully observed by many, and the church arose to new life and animation. During the interval of public worship on the Sabbath, meetings for prayer and exhortation were held at some of the neighboring dwelling houses. These were, even at first, attended by considerable numbers, and soon the principal part of the congregation were present. Serious inquiry respecting religion became extensively prevalent, and the evidence conclusive, that the Lord had revived his work among us. Religion and their own spiritual interests became the common topic of conversation among the people.

On the 1st of October our meeting-house was finished, and dedicated to God. Our meetings on Friday were then held there, no other place being sufficiently large to contain the assembly. We also had occasion to hold them each week, and to continue them from one o'clock till nearly sunset. The time was spent in prayer, in giving explanations of Scripture, and in addressing exhortations to the congregation. At these meetings candidates for admission into the church were examined. From one to ten came forward at a time, and on almost every Friday some were examined.

On the first Sabbath in September, 1813, some of the new converts were received into the church, and those received on the first Sabbath in September, 1814, with those who had been admitted during the past year, amounted to ninety-nine. There was one individual who had been propounded, who was unable, through indisposition, to attend public worship. At our next commemoration of our blessed Saviour's death, on the first Sabbath in November, that person and one other united with the church, making one hundred and one who were received in one year and two months. At our next sacramental season, on the first Sabbath in January, 1815, none were admitted into the church, and it was the first time that this was the fact, in eight such seasons. On this day, I administered the Lord's supper to upwards of two hundred communicants, most of whom were, by the grace of God, converted to Christ under my feeble ministry.

These are a few general outlines of the revival of religion in Bridport. I shall now enter upon a more extended detail of circumstances.

1. In our religious meetings, the doctrines insisted upon were the sovereignty of God, his purposes, total moral depravity, moral agency and accountableness, the circumstances which render human actions virtuous or vicious in the sight of God, justification solely by faith in Christ, the nature of saving faith and genuine repentance, the character of evangelical obedience, the obligations of men to do all they are able, just as much as if they could save them-

selves by their own works; the sure destruction of those who forbear all exertions, and of those also, who neglect to exert themselves in the right manner. These sentiments formed the general subject of the addresses at our meetings for religious services. They were, in a greater or less degree, exhibited whenever I was present, and I believe that they were uniformly declared throughout the town. I also noticed, that the more clearly those doctrines were brought forward, the more serious and profound was the attention of the audience, and the more salutary the effects which ensued.

Those who spoke in our meetings, did it usually in a low tone of voice, and with much deliberation, as if dealing out their ideas by items, that all might understand what was said.

Our conferences were generally dismissed by half past eight in the evening. Afterwards half an hour was often spent in conversing with individuals, and then all dispersed. When the assembly separated, they were particularly charged to proceed directly home, to read a portion of Scripture, and at times the passage was designated, and to pray to God in secret, before they retired to rest.

There was nothing at any time disorderly and vociferous. There were no outcries in our meetings, nor even a sob. But occasionally tears, both of joy and of sorrow, flowed freely.

It was made a point to inform no one that he had embraced religion. This subject was kept out of sight, that individuals might make the discovery for themselves. Those whose minds were affected, would often charge such as they conversed with to say nothing respecting them to others. Hence it did not spread from one to another, that individuals were under religious concern. In several instances persons came to my house to converse with me, of whom I did not previously know that their attention had been excited. Three lads from the lake shore, whom I did not even know, came in one day to converse with reference to uniting with the church. The first was but eleven years old. But he introduced himself like a man, and I was satisfied with the evidence which he exhibited that he possessed a vital acquaintance with religion. He has since been received as a member of the church.

2. In the examination of candidates for admission into the church, there was among

them all a uniformity of sentiment as to the purposes of God, election by grace, total depravity, the necessity of a real change of heart, in order to repentance, and faith in Christ, and the fact that this change is in answer to no prayer made by the subject before it takes place. In these particulars, all were so nearly alike, that a description of one would furnish an accurate representation of the rest. They were also harmonious in their views of the sanctity of the Sabbath, and the obligation of family and private devotion, and of household baptism. There were two persons who, for a number of years together, had been communicants in a Baptist church, who became convinced of their error, came forward and acknowledged it, united with the Congregational church, and in baptism dedicated their children to God. They are apparently pious, and are thoroughly convinced that they formerly labored under a mistake.

3. I shall now relate a few particulars of a miscellaneous character. They may not, however, be without interest in the view of the public.

At the time when the church came to a determination to renounce political conversation on the Sabbath, and also on other days, and engaged to observe a concert of prayer on Saturday evenings, there was a person present who has since declared, that when the church adopted these resolutions, it struck him that they had now commenced a course which would issue in a revival of religion among the people. It also occurred to him, that if he did not become a subject of divine grace in the season of attention which he anticipated, he should be left to final obduracy. For he was about thirty-six years of age, after which period of life, it is not frequently the fact that mankind are led to embrace religion. He informed us that these intimations rang in his ears, till he obtained a hope of an interest in the blessings of the gospel. He was previously full and decided in his belief of the doctrines of grace, and was not aware that he did not regard them with heartfelt approbation, or that there is a difference between believing the truth and regarding it with affection. But as soon as his feelings were touched, and his attention awakened, he discovered his mistake, and the discovery produced a distress, under which he labored for some time, as an insupportable burden. At length he obtained relief, and perceived in himself feelings towards the truths of Scripture, which he could not describe, and he now defends those truths from a reason which before had no existence in his breast. After a while, he informed us that he was constrained to call this new state of mind, Christian complacency in the great doctrines of the Bible. But how the change which he experienced, took place in his heart, which shortly before was full of opposition to those truths, he could not tell. He was sensible that his dislike had left him, and that a different feeling existed, and this was all he could say upon the subject. His wife was impressed with solicitude at the same time with himself. But for sometime they did not make known their feelings to each other. At length a disclosure was made, and they conversed with freedom. They both had one object of distress, the sovereignty of God, and his eternal purposes; yet they felt in a manner widely different on the subject. His agitation was occasioned by his finding in himself no cordial regard for those doctrines, though he firmly believed them. Her concern arose from fear that they were true, while she saw no evidence of their truth or propriety.

There was a man about forty-seven years of age, whose conversion was somewhat remarkable. His father died when he was very young. He was brought up in a very indifferent manner, and at an early period of life became addicted to vicious practices. He was notorious for profane swearing and intemperance. By his vices he had rendered himself not only useless, but even a burden to society. He was even a vagabond upon earth, and had sunk himself below the company of ordinary drunkards. He had no associates, but seemed a solitary being, almost shut out from society. His ordinary employment was serving as an hostler at the taverns in this town. He never, or at most, seldom went to meeting on the Sabbath, nor would he hear any religious conversation. If any person began to talk with him on serious subjects, he would directly withdraw, and use profane language respecting their hypocritical attempt, as he would term it. His habits of intemperance had reduced him to a very infirm state of health, and had rendered him an object odious and loathsome. At length he fell into a decline, and was obviously not far from the close of life. After the revival began, attempts were made to converse with him in reference to his spiritual interests, and his immortal welfare. But, for a while, every attempt was made in vain. He shortly became so ill that he did not go abroad, and but seldom left his room. He now became concerned respecting his salvation. With a Bible in his hand, he used to go from one to another, begging them to read to him, for he could scarcely, if at all, read himself, and entreating them to pray with him. He often said that he was afraid he should be lost, for he could neither read nor pray, and he had been so wicked, that he was apprehensive there was no mercy for him. His distress, at length, became so intense, that by means of it, in addition to his other complaint, he was wholly confined to his room, and most of the time to his bed. Now death appeared nigh, and his only prospect was that hell would be his final abode. This gave a keen edge to his distress, and when alone in his room, he began to cry aloud. The mistress of the house, hearing his voice, went to the door, it not being shut, and stood and listened to what he said, and was a witness of the scene which ensued. He began at his infancy, and confessed to God, first one sin, and prayed for repentance and forgiveness; and then he confessed another, and so on, till he had, in this manner, gone through the whole catalogue of his iniquities. He then summed up the whole in one mass, and prayed for mercy and deliverance. At length relief came, and the tears flowed, from a different cause from that which had before drawn them forth. His joy was so great, that he cried out in astonishment, "O, is this the case—can I be forgiven? Will that God receive me, whom I have so often offended, and whose wrath I so justly deserve?" All this took place in private, when he supposed that no one heard him, and that the whole transaction passed between only his God and himself. This frame of mind continued several days, with but little intermission. He asked every one that he thought had an interest at the throne of grace, to pray with him; and others he exhorted to repent and turn to God. He had an uncle, who was at the same time ill, and who came to his room to see the wonder, which drew the attention of all classes, religious and irreligious. He was in sentiment a fixed Universalist. As soon as he saw him, he cried out, "O, uncle, I have seen an end of the scheme which you have so often taught me. I pray you not to trust in it any longer." He had several prayers made in his room every day, by people of the town and by strangers. For all who visited us, went to see if the report concerning him was true, and they universally came away astonished, declaring it the work of the Lord. He continued much in the same state till he died, which was in about a month. He yielded up his life with great calmness, and with a strong hope of being with Jesus. His death seemed like that of Lazarus. He had no property. The family in which he died took suitable care of him, and gave him a decent burial, gratuitously. I preached at his funeral from Luke 16 : 22—"*And it came to pass that the beggar died, and was carried by angels into Abraham's bosom.*"

There was a young woman, who, on a sick-bed, the winter before the revival occurred, had obtained a hope that she had become a subject of divine grace. Her life was despaired of, and she was agitated by extreme anxiety and distress. At length she found relief, as she thought, by having recourse to the mercy revealed in the gospel, but did not expect that her life would be spared. She said much to her mates about death, and exhorted them to prepare for that awful event. After some time she began to recover, and by degrees entirely regained her health. Upon this, she grew remiss in her attention to religion, and seemed to have forgotten, in a great degree, her sick-bed vows. She was invited to a scene of gayety and amusement in the neighborhood. In the midst of the festivity and recreation, one of the party was seized with a fit, and was thought to be dying. This young woman was deeply impressed with alarm, and even horror, by this remarkable providence, and she told her companions that it was a judgment of God upon them for their folly and wickedness, and that they would die and perish forever, if they continued to neglect religion and provoke God. She now renounced her hope, and sunk into despair, viewing herself lost beyond recovery. In this state she continued several weeks. She was urged to resign herself unreservedly into the hands of God. She replied that she dared not do it, for he must deliver her over to perdition. At length her parents discovered an alteration in her feelings. They inquired respecting her state of mind, and she said she had surrendered herself to God. They asked her if she was not afraid that he would cast her off forever. She answered, that it appeared so just, that she must, even in that case, acquiesce.

There was a lad about fifteen years of age, who, when subject to religious anxiety, was afraid he could not be saved, for he could not pray, and he had no book from which he might learn. He said he thought the pious had a book from which they learned to pray, and that he did not know what he should do for a book, as he was poor, and could not buy one. He did not see but he must be lost because he could not pray. At length, however, he found that he did not need a book in order to learn to pray— that with a new heart, ability to pray is given— that with the spirit of grace, the spirit of supplication is imparted. He was asked with what denomination he intended to unite. His father was a member of a Baptist, but his mother of a Congregational church. By her he had been dedicated to God in baptism, and instructed in the principles and duties of religion. He replied that he should join the Congregational church; for he believed that God required parents to devote their children to him, and to teach them carefully the truths and duties of religion.

According to the best calculation which I can make, there have been one hundred and fifty souls hopefully born into the kingdom of Christ, during the late gracious visitation of heaven. One hundred and one have united with the church under my care; a few have joined the Baptist church, and others have, as yet, made no public profession of religion.

The Lord has dealt with us in wonderful mercy. The work which he has achieved, is one in which the Divine hand has been most clearly apparent. I rejoice that I have been the humble instrument which that glorious Being has employed to effect his benevolent designs; but the excellency of the power is of God.